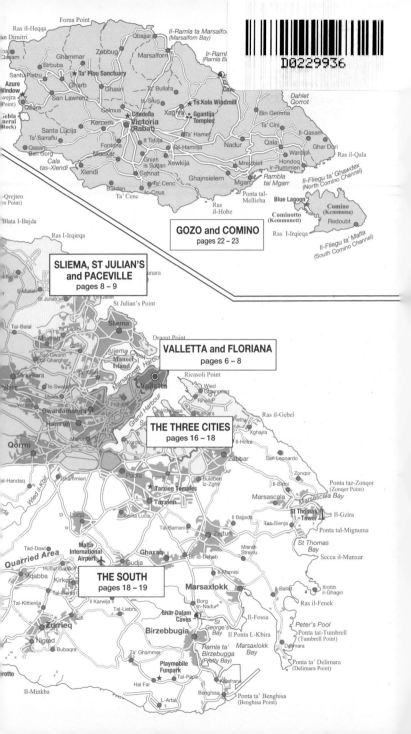

GOZO and COMINO
pages 22 – 23

SLIEMA, ST JULIAN'S and PACEVILLE
pages 8 – 9

VALLETTA and FLORIANA
pages 6 – 8

THE THREE CITIES
pages 16 – 18

THE SOUTH
pages 18 – 19

INSIGHT GUIDES

MALTA

Part of the Langenscheidt Publishing Group

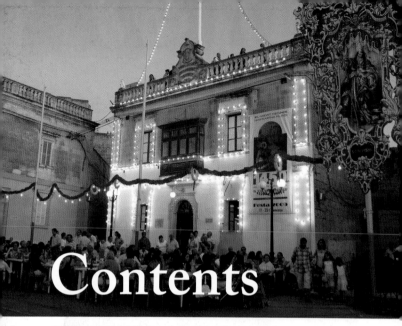

Contents

Highlights

▲ **The Blue Lagoon** Crystal clear waters and a tiny beach make Comino one of the most popular tourist spots. ▶ **Mdina** Trawl through the Silent City's quiet streets. Especially pleasant at night.

◀ **Temples** Unique throughout the world, Malta's Megalithic structures, such as Hagar Qim, date from 4000–2500 BC.

▲ **St John's Co-Cathedral** Ornate and interesting, the capital's cathedral is home to Caravaggio's largest ever painting.

▲ **Golden Bay** Malta's most popular sandy beach. Great for a spot of swimming, sunbathing or water sports.
◀ **Valletta** The historically rich capital is alive with characteristic backstreets, shops, cafes and great restaurants.

Malta

Thanks to their unmatched positioning smack-bang in the centre of the Mediterranean, the Maltese Islands have been a desirable location for centuries. Throughout that time unbridled passion and patriotism kept the islanders fighting for their independence. That zeal is still felt today and the result is a vibrant destination bubbling with culture, folklore, history and a cosmopolitan edge.

Malta Fact and Figures

Population: 405,165
Population density: 1,298 persons per sq km (3,321 persons per sq mile)
Total area: 316 sq km (122 sq miles)
Number of towns: 68
Official languages: Maltese, English
Religious affiliations: Roman Catholic 94 percent, nonreligious 1 percent, other 5 percent
Number of annual visitors: 1.2 million
Number of hotel and restaurants: 3,866
Number of museums: 70
Number of hills in Valletta: 7
Number of Islands: 7 (inhabited: 3)
National Anthem: Lil Din I-Art Helwa (Dedicated to this Sweet Land)

The Islands

Lying in the centre of the Mediterranean Sea (93km/57 miles south of Sicily and 288km/179 miles north of Africa), Malta, Gozo and Comino are the three main islands that constitute the Maltese Archipelago.

The islands' diverse and rich history has morphed them into a melting pot of cultures, traditions and attitudes which have long helped to bring tourists to the islands. Valletta – the capital, the Three Cities and Mdina are havens for history buffs, with their back streets and centuries-old architecture, much of it built by the Knights of the Order of St John during their possession of the islands during the 16th–18th centuries.

Not known as a beach destination, Malta does have some wonderful sandy beaches to enjoy, mostly in the north of Malta and on Gozo. Essentially it is Malta's lifestyle that foreigners are attracted to – long seaside promenades for leisurely strolls, great restaurants for lazy lunches and the omnipresent Mediterranean Sea that lulls backwards and forwards, ensuring tranquillity reigns despite the bustle found in the larger towns of these tiny islands.

The Islands' History

Malta has long been of strategic importance, but it was the Phoenicians who first realised this and occupied it. As it turned out, they were the first of many, followed in turn by the Greeks, Carthaginians, Romans, Normans and Arabs. The arrival of the Knights of St John, who obtained the islands from Charles V in 1530, was a vital landmark in the islands' history, and their presence can still be felt today in the beautiful palaces and fortifications that they left in their wake.

Sadly, a lot of Malta's most impressive architecture was damaged or destroyed dur-

Above: a future sailor in Marsaxlokk.

ing the First and Second World Wars, by which point the islands were under the rule of the British. Nevertheless the islands' eclectic historical past is still, especially so in Valletta, Mdina, the Three Cities and the Citadella in Gozo.

The Maltese People

Friendly, mostly English-speaking and vivacious, many Maltese will be thrilled to welcome you to their country and will often regale you with stories of its history as well as the best places to see, shop and dine during your visit. Listen to them; naturally exacting and for the most part traditional in their ways of life, they will often lead you to the off-the-beaten-track haunts that are a true traveller's dream.

That said, many Maltese are also fiercely protective of the islands they love – islands which they fear are now under threat from immigration, as Malta serves as a key EU processing centre for immigrants attempting to illegally cross the Mediterranean Sea from North Africa. Additionally, the years

Left: Sliema's The Victoria hotel, a luxurious retreat.

since Malta joined the EU have seen something of a brain drain take place, with many of its young people choosing to seek pastures greener and opportunities overseas.

What you will still find on the island is a pleasant mix of old-meets-new: bars in hundred-year-old houses, cafes slotted into bastions built by the Knights of St John and restaurants in seaside boathouses. It's this kind of eclecticism that runs through the islands and their people and you can certainly look forward to meeting a myriad of characters during your stay.

Visiting the Maltese Islands

Low-cost airlines have significantly pushed down the price of getting to Malta. Once here expect prices to be similar to mainland Europe, whether they're for sightseeing, wining and dining or accommodation.

The islands' main sights are spread all over, and the rickety public bus system (while on the up) is nothing to write home about, especially if you need to get anywhere by a particular time. Despite the fact that journeys are never more than 20 or so minutes long, it is advisable to hire a car to ensure you get the most out of your stay.

Valletta and Floriana

As a capital city Valletta may not be the cosmopolitan mecca many might expect, but it is full of eclecticism and charm. Built by the Knights of St John nearly five centuries ago, the whole region is now recognised as a World Heritage Site. A complete regeneration project is on the cards, revolving around the rebuilding of the bombed Opera House that has lain in ruins since the end of World War II, but spanning the whole city and due for completion by 2015. In the meantime, make the most of the picturesque backstreets, quaint cafés and wine bars, churches, museums and the stunning Waterfront promenade overlooking the Grand Harbour.

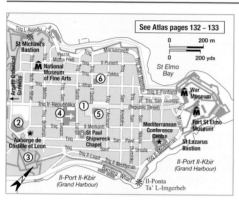

Above: memorial to the Great Siege of World War II.

THE CITY CENTRE

The hub of Valletta, **Republic Street** ① runs right across it, cutting through what is essentially the commercial and business district. Entering through City Gate and leaving the bustle of the bus station behind you, you can wander towards the **St James Cavalier Centre for Creativity** ②, which towers above Freedom Square. Built by the Knights of St John and restored at the turn of the millennium, this is now a hub for artsy types who love its old-meets-new vibe. Across from **Auberge de Castille et Leon**, the prime minister's base, sits

Upper Barrakka Gardens ③, a tranquil spot away from the city, perfect for taking pictures of the **Grand Harbour** below.

Something of a shopper's paradise, Republic Street is where you'll find recognisable international fashion brands and large complexes stocking anything and everything. Bear in mind that certain outlets close for a daily siesta

> **St Paul's Shipwreck Chapel**, tucked away on St John's Street, is off the tourist track and very tranquil. It is said to be home to one of St Paul's wrist bones. *See also Churches, p.44.*

between 1 and 4pm, although this is a tradition which is slowly dying out. Equally popular for shoppers, **Merchant's Street** was recently pedestrianised to make life easier for them. It has brought the street to life, and after the close of the sprightly morning *monti* (market), business people trawl the road for lunch-break bargains or an eatery to while away the hours. **St Lucy's Street**, one of the narrow backstreets, has long been the destination for jewellery shoppers, and specialised boutiques lie side by side.

History-lovers will be taken in by the magnitude of **St John's Co-**

Left: festa decorations in Valletta.

take in the stunning Grand Harbour vista. The **Mediterranean Conference Centre**, now a popular venue for theatregoers, was once the hospital of the Order of St John during their stay on the island. The audiovisual **Malta Experience** lies just across the road. Further down the coast, the **Valletta Waterfront** promenade has injected new life into this once forgotten part of town, as it is now awash with restaurants, cafés, shops and nightspots.

SEE ALSO ARCHITECTURE, P.28; CULTURAL ACTIVITIES, P.53; MUSEUMS, P.85

Cathedral ④ and what lies within its walls – including Caravaggio's largest ever painting, the *Beheading of St John*, which was completed in 1608. The **Grand Master's Palace** ⑤, overlooking the recently regenerated St George's Square, is equally rich and currently houses the valuable Gobelins tapestries woven in France for Grand Master Ramón Perellos y Roccaf, the **Armoury** and the island's Parliament.

Valletta remains the local capital for culture, and the majority of events take place within its fortified walls. The **Manoel Theatre** ⑥ is one of the city's gems and is reputed to be the third-oldest working theatre in Europe. Events are ongoing

Right: Upper Barrakka Gardens

through the year, and it's worth a visit just to sit in the auditorium to take in its three-tiered splendour.

SEE ALSO ARCHITECTURE, P.26; CHURCHES, P.44; CULTURAL ACTIVITIES, P.52, 53; MUSEUMS, P.84, 85; PARKS AND GARDENS, P.103

THE VALLETTA COAST

The waterfront region, though quite a walk to get to, is home to numerous gems and well worth the trek, especially as you

FLORIANA

Not particularly noted as a tourist destination, Floriana is a residential area just outside the capital. The **Argotti Botanical Gardens** are worth a visit if you have the time, as is the **Archipresbyterial Church of Floriana**, which is dedicated to Saint Publius, traditionally acclaimed as the first Bishop of Malta.

SEE ALSO PARKS AND GARDENS, P.102

Sliema, St Julian's & Paceville

If it's a faster pace you are after, this is where to find it. Originally a sleepy fishing village, this coastal region has morphed into Malta's shopping and entertainment district, with high-rise luxury buildings forever sprouting onto the skyline. Sliema has long been the chosen destination of the local IT crowd, who venture here to enjoy the typically Mediterranean café culture and international shopping brands. St Julian's, a short walk away along the picturesque promenade, is the leading destination for top-quality eateries, while Paceville is an entertainment hub with side-by-side clubs, pubs, bars and nightspots which stay lively until the early hours.

SLIEMA

Sliema is a busy town with pretty views across the bay to Valletta and Floriana. Located on a peninsula, it starts where Ta' Xbiex and Gzira end – but the three towns morph into each other so effortlessly that you would be forgiven for mistaking one for another.

The Sliema seaside promenade, nicknamed **The Ferries** ① and starting at the Manoel Island Marina, is a popular haunt for locals and tourists on evening walks. Numerous ships line the shore, and it is here that you can pick up a ferry over to Valletta – certainly the more leisurely way to travel to the city – or hop on a cruise around the islands.

The main road into Sliema is lined with restaurants offering international fare from Chinese to Indian and everything inbetween, as well as several moderately priced hotels. Once in the hub of the city, café culture takes hold, and there are numerous teashops and snack bars

Above: the calm waters of St George's Bay.

to choose from. This is also the island's shopping capital, where European fashion brands and complexes on **Tower Road** ② and **Bisazza Street** ③ vie with smaller, local boutiques on the side roads. Admittedly, a lot of traditional charm has been lost in Sliema, making way for a more modern way of life. Some magic has been retained in the less touristy parts of the town, its backstreets, where colourful town-houses and their eclectic residents still enjoy the status that comes from owning property in this area.
SEE ALSO BEACHES, BAYS AND PROMENADES P.38

ST JULIAN'S

Further north along the promenade Sliema

Map showing Sliema, St Julian's, Paceville and Gzira areas, including: St. George's Bay, Baystreet Shopping Complex, Il-Ponta tad-Dragunara, Dragonara Casino, Il-Qaliet, PACEVILLE, MEDITERRANEAN SEA, Spinola Palace, Il-Ponta Ta'Spinola, Spinola Bay ④, Il-Ponta Ta'San Giljan, St Julian's Tower, St. Julians, INDEPENDENCE GARDENS, Balluta Bay, ST JULIAN'S, Our Lady of Mt. Carmel, St Patricks, Sliema Point Tower, Il-Ponta Ta'Sliema, Stella Maris, Sacred Heart ③, Holy Trinity, GZIRA, SLIEMA ① ②, Valletta. Scale: 0–500 m / 0–500 yds.

Left: view from Balutta Bay.

SEE ALSO BEACHES, BAYS AND PROMENADES, P.40; PARKS AND GARDENS, P.103

PACEVILLE

Paceville is widely considered to be a playground for party animals, boasting a huge percentage of Malta's best pubs and clubs. During the day there is no getting away from the shabby feel that degrades its centre, so stick to the seaside and the newly regenerated **St George's Bay beach**. This small stretch of sand is manmade, creating the perfect pit stop for swimmers who relish its calm waters. Shoppers will also enjoy the **Baystreet Complex** just a moment's walk away, where various local and international stores, as well as cafés and restaurants, are spread over three floors.

At night Paceville finds its feet, and you can expect floods of people and plenty of heavy drinking. The town is extremely popular with the island's English students, who make it their home for the summer, as well as the locals who enjoy its cosmopolitan feel. For classier entertainment try the **Dragonara Casino** nearby.

SEE ALSO BEACHES, BAYS AND PROMENADES, P.38; SHOPPING, P.114

> For an authentic taste of the real Sliema head to the city's backstreets and keep your eyes peeled for traditional **closed timber balconies**, often painted in bright colours to match a home's front door. These balconies have been popular since the 18th century.

becomes St Julian's, and while there isn't a lot to do here during the day, it does come alive at night. Here Mediterranean living takes on a cosmopolitan feel, with plenty of chic hotels and nightspots.

St Julian's Tower, one of many built by the Knights of St John, serves as your entrance to the town, followed by the pretty **Independence Gardens** beneath the busy street.

Lovers of luxury living will feel most at home in St Julian's. The area boasts the majority of the island's five-star hotels, as well as many of its highly rated restaurants and bars. Despite the development surrounding it, **Spinola Bay** ④ retains plenty of its charm, as brightly coloured fishing boats *(luzzuz)* bob on the water and fairy lights illuminate the dock. You can even grab a gondola for a romantic trip out to sea. **Spinola Palace**, up the hill, is one of the region's only historic buildings and was built in 1688.

Mdina, Rabat and Dingli

Locals love this part of the island because it is a throwback to yester-year and a calm oasis rich in history and character. Mdina is a jewel – the oldest city on the island and one which dates back to pre-historic times. It is wonderful to walk through its Baroque streets, and many visitors choose to stop for a coffee in one of its bastion cafés that afford views over much of the island. The nearby town of Rabat is also charmingly traditional, and history buffs will love the stories behind its underground catacombs. Dingli is the island's highest point and offers stunning photo opportunities.

MDINA

Many call Mdina the Silent City, and at night you literally could hear a pin drop. Its name, derived from the word Medina, means city in Arabic, and it was under Arab rule that it took on much of the shape that we see today, although in a very different style. In 1530 the Knights of St John took hold of the islands and Mdina became their centre. After a strong earthquake in 1693, they rebuilt it in the Baroque design that it is still famed for today.

Enter through the main gate over the deep moat which is now a garden. Inside, cobbled streets

Left: St Paul in Rabat.

show the way to the city's prized site – the **Mdina Cathedral and Museum** ①, dedicated to the conversion of St Paul and fronted by a large square and two large cannons – the shiny subjects of many a photograph!

The amount of history here is staggering, so a second stop could be the **Mdina Experience** ②, a multilingual audio-visual presentation that will quickly bring you up to

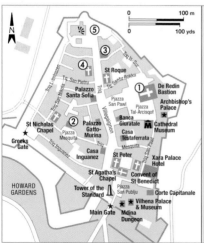

See Atlas page 134

Left and below: historic buildings of Mdina.

⑤ – a pretty square surrounded by Mdina's impressive walls – gives the opportunity to gaze down on most of the islands and is particularly scenic at night.
SEE ALSO ARCHITECTURE, P.29; CHURCHES, P.46; MUSEUMS, P.86; WALKS AND VIEWS, P.126

RABAT
Within easy walking distance, Rabat developed as a suburb to Mdina but is now a destination in its own right. Best known for its underground **catacombs**, dedicated to **St Paul** ⑥ and **St Agatha**, the **Roman Villa** also sits on the town's outskirts and ranks as having one of the oldest and best-preserved mosaic compositions in the western Mediterranean.
SEE ALSO MUSEUMS, P.87

DINGLI
Over 250m (800ft) above sea level, **Dingli Cliffs** ⑦ provide some of the most spectacular views in Malta, overlooking the open sea and the tiny, uninhabited island of Filfla. On the way, consider a stop at **Buskett Gardens**, Malta's only woodland area.
SEE ALSO PARKS AND GARDENS, P.102; WALKS AND VIEWS, P.126

Much of Malta has been used as a film set in recent years, and Mdina has proved particularly popular. The city has had roles in *The Count of Monte Cristo*, *Cutthroat Island*, TV opera film *The Death of Klinghoffer* and the BBC's 'Napoleon' for the series *Heroes and Villains*.

---

speed on all that you need to know about the city. Palaces, many now privately owned, lined the streets, but some have opened their doors to the public. A stunning example is the medieval **Palazzo Falson** ③, which has been lovingly restored and now hosts a fantastic collection of features and items from various stages in the city's history. Just across the road, the **Carmelite Church and Priory** ④ recently opened its doors

too, allowing for a sneak peek into the lives of the friars who have lived there for centuries.

Despite developing into a major tourist attraction today, Mdina still maintains its old-world charm. Just a handful of selected residents live within its walls, many of them with noble connections, and securing property here is both tough and expensive. As a final stop, **Bastion Square**

The Centre

Very much the island's middle ground, Malta's centre is a pleasing medley of residential, historic and traditional that begs exploration. There are few accommodation options in this area, but any you do find will be havens of tranquility well located off the standard tourist track. Saying that, the centre is home to a number of must-sees, including the Ta' Qali Crafts Village, where customary folklore practices are still on show daily, and the Mosta Dome, which survived a bomb attack in World War II. Sights are spread over a large area, so it is advisable to hire a car if you want to see this part of the island properly.

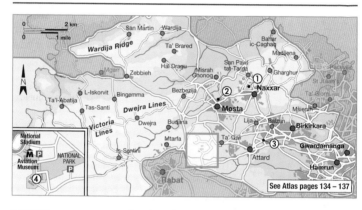

See Atlas pages 134 – 137

NAXXAR

Legend has it that the Naxxarin (inhabitants of this village) were some of the first to help St Paul after his shipwreck on the island, hence the little chapel dedicated to him on its outskirts. The expansive parish church, dedicated to **Our Lady of Victories**, was built in 1616 and remains the focus of this friendly village. The local council that manages Naxxar has made a real effort here, and it is often cleaner and greener than some of the others. A particularly pretty (but wholly residential) street is **St Lucy's**, which wings its way out of the parish centre to the outskirts.

The town's highlight is **Palazzo Parisio** ①, a 19th-century palace that has justifiably been called 'a miniature Versailles'. It has stayed in the same family for generations and is today run by Baroness Scicluna. An oasis of tranquillity, enjoy its lush gardens, tearoom (**Café Luna**) or fine dining restaurant (**Luna di Sera**).

SEE ALSO CAFÉS, P.35; MUSEUMS, P.87; PARKS AND GARDENS, P.103; RESTAURANTS, P.110

MOSTA

Busy and bustling, Mosta is probably the commercial capital of this central region, and its main road, Constitution Street, is lined with shops, restaurants and bars. The town's claim to fame is the miraculous bombing of its parish church in 1942, when an Axis bomb pierced **Mosta**

Right: Palazzo Parisio.

Left: San Anton Gardens.

dent's official residence.
SEE ALSO PARKS AND GARDENS,
P.103

TA' QALI
What used to be an RAF station during World War II is now a recreational area with plenty of roaming space. The **Malta Aviation Museum** within the park's boundaries recollects the old days.

Tourists will enjoy the **Ta' Qali Crafts Village** ④, home to many of Malta's craftsmen. Most factories here welcome tourists, and you will be able to glimpse practices including glassblowing and pottery-making before moving on to their outlets.

Nearby, **Ta' Qali National Park** has become popular for outdoor theatre and concerts; parts of it are currently undergoing a revamp, so access may be limited.
SEE ALSO MUSEUMS, P.87; PARKS AND GARDENS, P.103; SHOPPING, P.114

If a typical *pjazza* and quaint backstreets are what you are looking for, head to nearby **Balzan** or **Lija**. If you happen to make it to Lija's annual *festa* (held on and around 6 August), don't miss the massive fireworks display – one of the island's most popular.

Attard enjoy the tranquillity of **San Anton Gardens** ③. Open to the public since 1882, these formal gardens make for a lovely stroll, coupled with the unbeatable backdrop of **San Anton Palace**, the presi-

Dome ② in the **Church of the Assumption** during a religious mass but failed to explode. A replica of the bomb is now displayed as a memorial. The unsupported dome is, in itself, another site to behold – one of the largest in world, it took 27 years to complete.
SEE ALSO CHURCHES, P.47

ATTARD
Peaceful and pleasant, Attard is one of the newer towns in Malta. While in

Right: Mosta Dome.

Bahar ic-Caghaq, Bugibba and St Paul's Bay

This coastal expanse of land is always bustling. Bahar ic-Caghaq is noteworthy for its two parks – one is Malta's only water park and the other its only animal park. Bugibba is now the island's largest tourist resort, with a taste of Britain thanks to the array of pubs and nightspots and a beautiful promenade to wander along. St Paul's Bay is its sleepier sister, with a more peaceful and untouched approach to life. The region's population skyrockets from 14,000 people in the winter months to some 60,000 during summer.

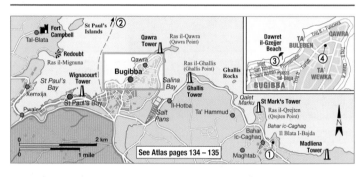

See Atlas pages 134 – 135

BAHAR IC-CAGHAQ

Situated on the mouth of Malta's longest valley, Bahar ic-Caghaq literally translates as Bay of Pebbles, so called because of its rocky terrain. During the British colonial period it served as the forces' campsite. Today leisure is of paramount importance here, and the town is home to two of the island's most popular attractions – the **Splash and Fun Water Park** ① and the **Mediterraneo Marine Park** ②. Each provide good, family fun and full days out; the latter is the only spot in Malta where you can swim with dolphins, but it is paramount to book ahead

Right: Splash and Fun Water Park.

especially during the chock-a- block summer months.

If all that action isn't your thing, the **Bahar ic-Caghaq Bay** makes for a nice coastal walk, and one of the island's best ice-cream trucks awaits on

your return.

SEE ALSO CHILDREN, P.42

BUGIBBA

This once sleepy seaside village lay virtually uninhabited until the 60s, when businessmen saw its potential and built hotels to entice tourists to it. Since then the development here has been phenomenal, and it is now home to numerous large hotels and resorts as well as umpteen restaurants, bars and nightclubs. Many locals also choose to have a holiday home here and use it as their base for the hotter months. Sadly, over the years little regard was given to the region's appearance, and much of it is a hotchpotch of styles that jar on the skyline.

Left: hitting the beach near Bugibba.

here. One of them, the **Malta Classic Car Museum** ④, has fast become a must-see with over 50 examples of classic vehicles that enthusiasts will love. Expect shopping in Bugibba to be typically touristy, with a vast array of souvenir shops to choose from and plenty of stalls selling handmade jewellery and other trinkets.

SEE ALSO BEACHES, BAYS AND PROMENADES P.39; MUSEUMS, P.88

ST PAUL'S BAY

St Paul's Bay is said to be the landing point of Malta's patron Saint Paul when he was shipwrecked on the island in AD 60, as documented in the Bible. Calmer than its touristy neighbour, this town is a nice window on a more typical way of life. **Wignacourt Tower**, built by Grand Master Wignacourt in 1610, is probably the most noteworthy historic building found here, and now hosts an exhibition of the knight's fortifications.

St Paul's shipwreck, nearly 2,000 years ago, marked the birth of Christianity on the Maltese Islands. Legend has it that **St Paul** was on his way to Rome to be tried as a political rebel when his boat was washed ashore. It is suggested that he landed on the islet now known as St Paul's Island, across from St Paul's Bay, and a statue stands there in his honour. A new viewing spot on the St Paul's Bay Bypass is perfect for taking pictures of this deserted island.

world go by. Beneath the promenade, a new manicured and manmade sandy beach known as **Dawret il-Gzejjer**, has increased the region's popularity as a swimming spot, though locals tend to prefer the rockier areas further along the road.

More and more attractions are mushrooming

Thankfully the government has put a facelift plan into action and it is starting to take shape. **Islet Promenade** ③, now lined with palm trees, makes for a pretty evening stroll, and Bay Square is a great place to sit and watch the

Right: St Paul's Bay.

15

The Three Cities

Collectively called Cottonera, the Three Cities are made up of Cospicua, Vittoriosa and Senglea, all of which were fortified by the Knights of St John. They make up part of the area surrounding Malta's world-renowned Grand Harbour. Cospicua is the largest and became known for its docks, which were built in 1776 and marked a turning point in the town's history. Vittoriosa is, today, the most picturesque of the trio, with bars and restaurants along its modern marina. Senglea is best known for withstanding the Ottoman invasion during the Great Siege and remains fiercely proud of that fact. If you love history, no trip to Malta is complete without a visit here.

COSPICUA

With charming backstreets to explore and history in abundance, Cospicua is full of passion and a great place to spend an afternoon. Inhabited since Neolithic times, it was the last of the Three Cities to be fortified; the Knights of St John made up for this, though, and by the middle of the 18th century it was declared a city in its own right by Grand Master Zondadari.

Famed for its dockyards, plans are now under way to regenerate the town completely. Until then, make the most of its historical and religious sites, including the

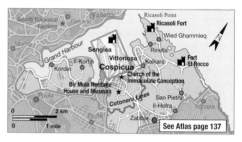

lavish **Church of the Immaculate Conception**, **Vilhena Gate**, the **Bir Mula Heritage House and Museum**, as well as its backstreets and alleys.
SEE ALSO ARCHITECTURE, P.26; CHURCHES, P.48

VITTORIOSA

The Knights chose Vittoriosa as their first capital city before later opting to build Valletta across the harbour. With **Fort St Angelo** at its tip, the city

became their headquarters and living quarters, even withstanding the terror of the Great Siege. While parts of the fort are closed to the public, many are open for exploration.

The **Inquisitor's Palace** ① is one of the highlights of the region. It is rumoured to be one of the few surviving palaces of the Roman Inquisition that were once widespread through Europe and the Roman Catholic world. A range of cells still

Left: Vittoriosa Waterfront.

traditional fishing boats.
SEE ALSO ARCHITECTURE, P.27;
BEACHES, BAYS AND PROMENADES,
P.41; MUSEUMS, P.88

SENGLEA

Developed by Grand Master de la Sengle, who fortified it following the Turk's invasion, this town has grown into a vibrant enclave. With an area of just over half a square mile, it is Malta's smallest locality. The town's pride and joy is the **Maria Bambina Basilica** ④, which boasts an almost unparalleled collection of religious treasures and artefacts, as well as the miraculous statue of *Jesus the Redeemer*, which is said to have healing powers.

A pretty photo spot, the **Gardjola Gardens** enjoy panoramic views that include the docks in Marsa, Valletta, the entrance to the Grand Harbour and Fort St Angelo.
SEE ALSO CHURCHES, P.48; PARKS AND GARDENS, P.102

A particularly devout area, the Three Cities are known for their **religious feasts**, so catch one if you can. The run-up to Easter is of particular local importance, and Holy Week commences with the sombre Good Friday procession. Things take on a completely different feel when the bells toll merrily to celebrate Easter Sunday.

Waterfront ③ makes a wonderful pitstop between sites. Having been lovingly restored in recent years, the marina and restaurant-bedecked promenade make for a lovely walk, surrounded by yachts and

boast original inscriptions dating back centuries, and another notable feature is the well-preserved sanitation system, which was certainly ahead of its time. The **Malta Maritime Museum** ② nearby is an interesting tribute to the harbour town.

There is no doubt that history is the main reason to come to the Three Cities, but the **Vittoriosa**

Left and Right: Fort St Angelo – the Knights kept an eye on everything.

The South

Malta's southern half comprises several smaller villages where life is reminiscent of former days. Traditional practices still dominate everyday life, and there is a laid-back, Mediterranean way of living that puts more emphasis on the home. Marsaxlokk, a busy seaside town, is particularly popular for its Sunday fish market, while nearby Marsascala offers a delightful promenade with plenty of quiet spots to while away the hours. If you have hired a car, take the time to drive off the main roads to explore the smaller villages en route; many of them offer a window onto the past and the real Malta.

Left: Birzebbugia's Pretty Bay.

MARSAXLOKK

Marsaxlokk Bay is the island's second-largest natural harbour and an active fishing village. Sunday morning is the best, and busiest, time to visit if you want to witness the hustle and bustle of the town's weekly **fish market** ①. Here stalls brim over with the freshest catch, some of which is instantly sold off to the nearby fish restaurants. Get ready to haggle for anything you want!

If you've missed the market you can still enjoy the peaceful promenade overlooking the bay. It was here that the Ottoman Turks landed, sparking the Great Siege of 1565. All memory of that has been wiped out, however, leaving in its wake the brightly coloured, bobbing fishing boats and a sense of calm tranquillity.
SEE ALSO FOOD AND DRINK, P.70

MARSASCALA

Another pretty bay, Marsascala is the summer holiday spot of choice for many southern residents as well as tourists. Historic-ally speaking, the village is quite rich. **St Thomas Tower**, in St Thomas Bay, was built by Grand Master Wignacourt following an attack on the village, while **Mamo Tower**, on the road leading to Zejtun, was built in 1657 to add further protection to the region.

Today the whole area is awash with little pubs and restaurants, and also offers some great walking opportunities.

BIRZEBBUGIA

The home of Malta's Freeport, Birzebbugia has relinquished a lot of its natural charm to this sprawling sea development. **Pretty Bay**, a clean

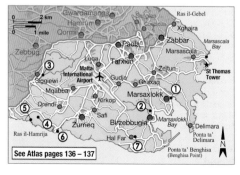

See Atlas pages 136 – 137

Left: traditional boats at Birzebbugia.

world's most important Megalithic temples – the 5,000-year old **Hagar Qim** ④. It is one of several temples still preserved on the island, including the **Mnajdra Temples** ⑤ a short walk away and the neighbouring **Tarxien Temples**. Hagar Qim is said to be the best preserved of the lot, and probably dates back to 3600 BC.

Nearby in **Wied iz-Zurrieq**, the **Blue Grotto** ⑥ is one of the most stunning and picturesque parts of Malta. One of a number of caves, it can be reached by boat. Be on the lookout for the brilliant phosphorescent colours of the underwater flora, as well as the views of Filfla, one of Malta's uninhabited islands.
SEE ALSO TEMPLES, P.121

HAL-FAR
Beyond the airport, Hal-Far is a stretch of industrialised land not usually frequented by tourists. The only noted place of interest is the **Playmobile Funpark & Factory**, which offers families a great day out as they watch these beloved toys come to life.
SEE ALSO CHILDREN, P.42

While the centre of Malta is predominantly English-speaking, Maltese is more widely spoken in the south. Here life also tends to be less cosmopolitan, with lifestyles harking back to a more traditional style and pace.

and sandy stretch, is otherwise attractive, as is the surrounding countryside. The area is most noted for the **Ghar Dalam Caves** ②, the earliest evidence of settlement in Malta dating back some 7,400 years.
SEE ALSO BEACHES, BAYS AND PROMENADES, P.37; TEMPLES, P.120

SIGGIEWI
This traditional village is worth a visit, with a myriad of tiny streets leading from the central *pjazza* and

parish church, and plenty of charm to boot. The **Limestone Heritage** ③, on its outskirts, is its most popular attraction. This family-run exhibition celebrates one of Malta's main resources – its stone. Set in a disused quarry, it makes for a great family day out.

QRENDI, ZURRIEQ AND TARXIEN
The tiny village of **Qrendi** is home to one of the

Right: Marsaxlokk fish market.

The North

Fast gaining popularity as a more low-key tourist destination, the north is home to some of Malta's most stunning vistas, best beaches, top resorts and renowned restaurants. Its topography includes cliffs, valleys, green fields and tiny bays, and despite recent development here, it still makes a welcome break from the more concrete parts of the island. Xemxija is a picturesque inlet, known for its restaurants and tiny promenade. The Golden Bay region boasts two of Malta's best beaches, as well as stunning views out to sea. Mellieha, a traditional village with a touristy feel, is arguably the capital of the north, with plenty to see and do, as well as another popular sandy beach.

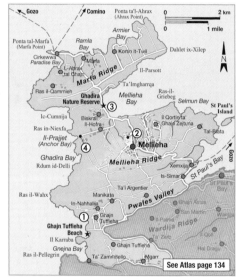

XEMXIJA

En route to many of the island's hotspots, Xemxija is a drive-by destination that may escape you. A good base, it is a gateway to the north's best beaches and villages, as well as the ferry terminal over to Gozo.

Perfectly suited to those after the quieter things in life, you will still find some good hotels and restaurants here, as well as some fantastic walks through the countryside. Locals often stop by the Xemxija Bay vegetable truck to pick up fresh produce, or stop to linger over an ice cream before continuing on to their destination.

GOLDEN BAY AND GHAJN TUFFIEHA

This part of Malta revolves around its beaches. Idyllically set between untouched and dramatic cliff faces and the open sea, **Golden Bay** ① is probably Malta's most popular sandy beach. The sand is, as suggested, golden and fine, and the stretch of space available means there is plenty of room for lounging or

games. The sea here is safe – though do keep your eyes peeled for jellyfish – and a red flag will indicate when it is only advised to stay in the shallow waters. Up on land, the region is home to one of the island's most popular five-star hotels, and numerous activities including horse riding and countryside walks.

A 10-minute walk away, **Ghajn Tuffieha** (the

Left: Red Tower, Marfa Ridge.

MELLIEHA

Easily the largest town in the region, Mellieha looks directly out over Malta's sister islands Comino and Gozo; in fact it's here that you'll need to get to in order to catch the ferry to either sister island.

Originally ignored as a location for fear of invasion by the corsairs, Mellieha was first developed by the British, and it has since flourished into a pretty town surrounded by sub-urbs and villas. It offers tourists the chance to explore its busy centre, the lavish **Nativity of the Virgin Mary Church** ②, unobstructed views and **Mellieha Beach** ③ – another of the most popular ones on the island. It is a good seaside base for those keen to spend time on the beach, and the **Popeye Village** ④ – a great day out for all ages – is within easy reach too.
SEE ALSO BEACHES, BAYS AND PROMENADES, P.36; CHILDREN, P.42, 43; CHURCHES, P.49

Bird-hunting is high on the list of contentious local issues – the hunters argue that it is a vital part of their heritage, while bird-lovers are keen to protect the many species that fly over the islands during the migration season. The wetland **Ghadira Nature Reserve**, behind Mellieha Beach, is a haven for birds that stop by for a drink and a rest, though it is not currently open to the public.

ral. And it looks set to stay that way thanks to an initiative by the local Gaia Foundation, which is now managing its well-being and upkeep on behalf of the government.
SEE ALSO BEACHES, BAYS AND PROMENADES, P.36

Apple's Eye) is another sandy beach. Slightly harder to get to, it is less popular with families and more so with young people keen to see or be seen, and holidaymakers after a less mainstream spot on the sand. Reached after a climb down 180 stairs (never mind the trek back up), it is unspoilt and natu-

Right and above left:
Popeye Village.

Gozo and Comino

Malta's two sister islands, Gozo and Comino, enjoy a far slower tempo and laid-back aura than Malta itself. Visitors often comment that a trip to Gozo feels like a step back in time, where traditional customs are still practised on a daily basis and life is wholly focused on the family. That said, modernity is starting to make inroads, with international stores, posh eateries and vibrant nightspots springing up to serve international visitors. Comino, on the other hand, is as close to a deserted island as you can get in these parts, with a permanent population of just four and some stunning, untouched scenery.

GOZO

Nicknamed the Isle of Calypso, Gozo has a population of just 31,000. Popular with day-trippers who take the 25-minute car ferry over to Mgarr Harbour, it has now become a destination in its own right, with several world-class accommodation options, great restaurants, shops and a nightlife all of its own.

The capital, **Victoria** ①, is vibrant and full of charm, with numerous pleasant options for whiling away the hours. **Fortunato Mizzi Street** runs right through it, with shops and complexes on both sides. The Old Town, built around the parish church, is a maze of tiny streets, little boutiques and religious shrines. The village square, known as **it-Tokk**, is a great spot for

> Gozo has topped several polls in its time, scoring within the top five in surveys of the world's best dive spots, places to live and places that make you happy. Whatever it is, there's certainly something in the air or the water that sees visitors returning year after year, some of whom even settle on the island.

watching the world go by, and a sprightly morning market takes place here most days.

On the hill above the capital looms the walled **Citadella**, first fortified during the Bronze Age. With panoramic views of the whole island, it is worth the climb, and there is plenty to do once you get inside – from a visit to **Gozo Cathedral**, to the **Old Prison** or the **Natural Science Museum**.

Said to be the spot where Odysseus was imprisoned, **Calypso's Cave** ② is another one of Gozo's must-sees. Just a

Left: the narrow streets of Victoria.

SEE ALSO ARCHITECTURE, P.27; BEACHES, BAYS AND PROMENADES, P.38; CHURCHES, P.49; MUSEUMS, P.89, 91; TEMPLES, P.120; WALKS AND VIEWS, P.125, 126

COMINO

A couple of times a day a little ferry takes visitors to Comino situated right between Malta and Gozo, or you could choose to go there as part of a boat trip around the three islands. Completely untouched during the winter months, throngs of visitors make space something of a premium during the summer as they vie for a sunbathing spot on the tiny beach. Swimmers love the crystal-clear waters of the **Blue Lagoon** ⑦, and the rest of the island makes for a lovely walk if the sun isn't beating down. Look out for Comino's tiny chapel, which dates back to 1618.

SEE ALSO BEACHES, BAYS AND PROMENADES, P.36

short distance from the pretty village of **Xaghra**, expect quite a climb, but a view that is well worth it. **Ramla Bay** ③, below, with its bright red sand, is Gozo's most popular sandy beach and a safe haven for families thanks to its shallow waters. Within easy reach are the **Ggantija Temples** ④, a Unesco World Heritage Site and some of the oldest religious structures in the world.

On the other side of the island, the 50m (164ft) high rock arch known as the **Azure Window** and the **Dwejra Inland Sea** ⑤ are magnificent geological features, popular with divers. You can also take a little boat out to admire the cliffs and caves from a different angle. The quaint village of **San Lawrenz** nearby makes for a nice coffee stop en route.

Other unmissable spots in Gozo include the **Ta Pinu Shrine**, the seaside villages of **Xlendi** and **Marsalforn**, and the **Fontana Springs**.

Right: the dramatic cliffs of Gozo.

A–Z

In the following section Malta, Gozo and Comino's attractions are organised by theme, under alphabetical headings. Items that link to another theme are cross-referenced. All sights that are plotted on the atlas section at the end of the book are given a page number and grid reference.

Architecture

Architecture in Malta is a bit of a mishmash, with styles jarring as they meet on the skyline. Enthusiasts will enjoy Valletta, where numerous structures built by the Knights still stand, dwarfing their more modern counterparts. Valletta is currently in the throes of a massive makeover, scheduled for completion by 2015, which will revamp many of its tired buildings, including the bombed Opera House site. Across the rest of the islands, old battles against new, especially on the coast where high-rise apartments have taken over. Look out for the architectural diamonds in the rough, some of them old, some of them new.

Auberge de Castille et Leon

St Paul's Street, Valletta; tel: 2200 1852; all buses to Valletta; map p.132 B1

Currently the prime minister's office and closed to the public, this 18th-century Baroque structure is best absorbed from the outside. Originally designed in 1574 by Gerolamo Cassar, in 1744 it saw extensive renovations by Domenico Cachia. Approached by a grand staircase and cannons dating from 1756, the masterful doorway features the bust of Pinto amidst the flags.

Gerolamo Cassar was the first local person who worked as an architect, and he had a great impact on the development of the island. Throughout his career, Cassar designed the auberges for several different langues of the Order, the Grand Master's Palace, the Convent Church and numerous other churches in Valletta.

Basilica of St George

Charity Street, Victoria, Gozo; tel: 2155 6377; www.stgeorge.org.mt; daily 4.45am–8pm; map p.132 B1

This church is core to Gozo's early Christianity, with St George symbolising the island's joining of faith with Malta. The foundation stone, laid in 1672, is entirely covered in marble, hence its title of 'the marble basilica'. Step inside to admire the gilded bronze canopy over the high altar, with paintings in the ceiling and dome featuring Giovanni Battista Conti of Rome.

Church of the Immaculate Conception

65, Triq il-Genduz, Cospicua; tel: 2182 2843; www.cospicuaparish.org.mt; Tue, Thur 4.30–6pm, Sat 10–11am; map p.135 E1

Dedicated to the Immaculate Conception and elevated in 1822, the church houses a statue of the Virgin Mary; originally carved from wood in the 17th century, crowned by Cardinal Ferrata in 1905 and adorned with a halo of 12 stars, 50 years later, by Cardinal Tedeschini. This richly furnished church hosts the splendid annual Feast of the Immaculate Conception on 8 December.

Right: Fort St Angelo, built to protect the peninsula of Valetta.

Left: Auberge de Castille et Leon.

Mare, meaning fort by the sea, this majestic castle was associated with the noble Maltese families of Guevara and De Nava, then later handed over to the Order of St John in 1530. The medieval Maltese architecture is Norman in style and owes its formidable appearance to the military engineers of the Order.

Inquisitor's Palace
Main Gate Street, Vittoriosa; tel: 2182 7006; 9am–4pm; any bus to Valletta, change to Vittoriosa; map p.135 E1
This is one of the few remaining inquisitor's palaces in Europe, used formerly for the established inquisition in Malta in 1574. The interior, despite being simple in its decoration, is home to some period furniture pieces, which add an original 16th-century touch in the restored Italian-style architecture. Inside you

The Citadella
Victoria, Gozo; tel: 2156 2034; 9am–4pm; map p.138 B3
Situated on a strategic vantage point in Gozo, this formidable castle dominates Victoria's skyline with its military presence. The north side dates to the Aragonese domination period, while the south was rebuilt between 1599 and 1603

by the Knights of St John. The tiring walk up Castle Street is forgotten when the Citadel archway welcomes your eyes to the impressive Gozo Cathedral and panoramic views of valleys and villages.

Fort St Angelo
Birgu; map p.135 E1
Formerly known by the Italian name of Castello a

Architecture

27

The islands' **prehistoric temples** are perhaps the greatest feats of architecture that grace the Maltese landscape. They can be viewed as the earliest surviving instance of the use of local limestone, the soft yellow stone that is still utilised by the building industry today. *See also Temles, p.120–1*

can discover the living quarters of the inquisitor, the prison cells and the courtrooms.
SEE ALSO MUSEUMS, P.88

Manikata Church
Shalom, Triq il-Mejjiesa, Manikata; tel: 2157 5679; Thur–Mon 5–7pm, Tues–Wed 6.30am–7pm; map p.134 B5
Formerly the old chapel of

St Joseph, prominent Maltese architect Richard England designed this larger church in 1961 better to accommodate the Manikata community. The stone used in construction was chosen specifically. To construct the screen wall behind the altar, stone was brought from the local fields and quarries west of Mgarr. In 1974 Archbishop Sir Michael Gonzi blessed the church 10 years after he had laid the first stone. Architect England has designed numerous other buildings and monuments in Malta, including the infamous LOVE statue in St Julian's, the university and the revamp of the St James Cavalier Centre for Creativity *(see p.53)*.

Right: the impressive dome of St Paul's. **Below:** Selmun Palace, built for the Knights of St John.

Mediterranean Conference Centre
Valletta; tel: 2124 3840; any bus to Valletta; map p.133 D3
The centre was originally the *Sacra Infermeria*, or Holy Infirmary, of the Order of St John. Constructed towards the end of the 16th century, this architectural landmark was transformed into a business centre in 1979, tastefully combining modern technology with ancient tranquillity. Comprising 10 large rooms, the centre boasts one of the longest halls in Europe, originally the

Long Ward of the infirmary and an architectural feat.
SEE ALSO CULTURAL ACTIVITIES, P.53

Palazzo Falson

Villegaignon Street, Mdina; tel: 2145 4512; www.palazzo falson.com; Tue–Sun 10am–5pm; bus: 80, 81, 84; map p.134 C1

This medieval palace evokes Sicilian inspiration, consisting of rooms entwined around a central courtyard, with the oldest part of the house dating back to the 13th century. Once home to Capt Olof Frederick Gollocher OBE (1889–1962) and his extensive collection of art and historical objects, the Palazzo has been fully restored, providing a unique house of delights, and architectural feats, to the general public.
SEE ALSO MUSEUMS, P.86

St Lawrence Church

91, St Lawrence Street, Vittoriosa; tel: 2182 7057; map p.135 E1

The foundation stone of this church was laid by Bishop Michele Giloramo Molina in 1681 and construction was completed in 1696. Inside it is richly decorated, featuring a myriad of paintings and sculptures. World War II damage destroyed important documents left by the Knights, who were served by the church for 41 years, and also the main dome, rendering the church out of use in 1942. The dome was rebuilt by Professor Robert V Galea in 1952.
SEE ALSO CHURCHES, P.48

St Paul's Cathedral

St Paul's Square, Rabat; tel: 2145 4136; map p.134 C1

Designed by Lorenzo Gafa, the cathedral is a stunning replacement for a ruined Norman cathedral, crushed in the 1693 Malta earthquake. However, recovered artefacts such as the painting by Calabrian artist Mattia Preti depicting the conversion of St Paul and a 15th-century Tuscan painting of the Madonna and Child remain – a hint of the previous cathedral. Once inside you won't find an inch of wall that isn't bedecked in either gold, paintings or red satin.

Selmun Palace

Selmun l/o Mellieha; tel: 2152 1040; map p.134 B3

Built in 1783 for the Knights of St John's Order, the original 18th-century architectural design by Domenico Cachia is culturally enchanting. A landmark in the village of Selmun, it features one of the largest towers to be built by the Order. This majestic castle, located in the north of the island, is a historical treat for culture-seekers.

29

Bars and Cafés

Café culture is rife in Malta, and locals love nothing more than to sit back with a cup of something warm and watch the world go by. Sliema is the obvious choice if you want to immerse yourself in this aspect of Mediterranean living, as little cafés – many with free Wifi – are dotted along the coast offering ideal spots for people-watching. The island's bars are a mix of chic lounges, serving delightful cocktails and pre-dinner drinks, and charming wine taverns set in centuries-old buildings within village backstreets. Both are ideal for friendly catch-ups or mixing with the locals. *See also Nightlife, p.92–7.*

BARS

VALLETTA

Legligin
119, St Lucy's Street; tel: 2122 1699; daily until late with exceptions; map p.132 B2
Head down the steep staircase into this attractive and inviting basement wine bar just round the corner from the Manoel Theatre. The wine list is extensive and bottles are chilled rather innovatively – in holes in the wall. The menu is enticing, too, with tapas treats including cheeses, hams and juicy fresh prawns.

The Pub
136, Archbishop's Street; tel: 2124 1655; daily until late; map p.133 C2
This small, English-style pub is best known for being the place where actor Oliver Reed died close to the final filming days of the blockbuster *Gladiator*. Now known as 'Ollie's Last Pub', it is a tribute to him, with scenes from his films and news-

Above: cider and other English fare feature at The Pub.

paper articles filling the walls. Aside from well-priced drinks at the bar, you can also buy T-shirts of a laughing Oliver Reed.

Trabixu Wine Bar
1, Strait Street; tel: 2122 3346; Tue–Fri noon–2.30pm, Tue–Sat 7pm–1am; map p.132 C3
A super spot for post-theatre or after-dinner drinks. Relax downstairs or on the tiny tables outside, enjoying the reasonably priced plonk and delicious bar menu which includes daily specials such as platters and shepherd's pie.

Locals love it, so get there early before all the best tables are taken.

SLIEMA, ST JULIAN'S AND PACEVILLE

Bar Native
St Rita's Steps, St George's Road, Paceville; tel: 2138 0635; daily 7am–4pm; map p.135 E2
Unwind perched on the outdoor terrace or in the air-conditioned indoor seating area, enjoying the wide choice of local and foreign beers and cider. Banter with friends or relax while listening to soft background music; things do tend to liven up considerably as the evening wears on.

Bianco's
21, St George's Road, St Julian's; tel: 2135 9865; www.biancos.info; daily noon–late; map p.135 D2
A chic new hangout loved by the local IT crowd. Kick back on the comfortable sofas or sit nearer the bar, while enjoying splendid views of Spinola Bay as you sip a glass of fine wine.

Left: café life is popular with the Maltese and the easiest way for tourists to experience local life.

nove.com; daily noon–late; map p.135 D2

A contemporary and casual wine and food concept-café overlooking picturesque Spinola Bay. Daily specials suit different tastes with Tuesday mussel nights, curry Thursdays and set lunch menus. Wednesdays are reserved for weekly wine-tasting.

MDINA, RABAT, DINGLI

Tat-Tarag
21, Saqqaja Hill, Rabat; tel: 2145 3088; www.tat-tarag.com; 7pm–midnight; map p.134 C1
Unwind within walls that feature bright paintings and mirrors, with breath-taking views, quality wine and tasty dips. This place stocks the finest wines from five continents, chosen by wine experts, so connoisseurs will feel right at home.

The **drinking age** in Malta was recently raised from 16 to 17. But even though this law is rarely enforced by bartenders and bouncers, it's best to carry ID with you at all times, just in case.

friends, enjoying the background music and buzzing atmosphere. Grab a drink in the chic lounge or sit street-side, watching as the party atmosphere hots up outside.

Nove Wine & Beer Bar
St George's Road, St Julian's; tel: 2137 5448; www.chillat

BJ's
Ball Street, Paceville; tel: 2133 7642; 8pm–late; map p.135 E2
Tucked away from the busy streets of Paceville this place tends to attract a more mature crowd. Enjoy daily live music daily, featuring well known local and international bands, and plenty of jazz. Live music starts at midnight.

Hugo's Lounge
St Rita's Steps, St George's Road, Paceville; tel: 2138 3639; www.hugosloungemalta.com; Mon–Thur noon–1am, Fri–Sun noon–3am; map p.135 E2
One of the best outlets in the Paceville region, this sushi-noodle bar is the ideal spot to relax with

Right: the basement bar, Legligin.

THE CENTRE

Fra Giuseppe

3, Triq Dun Spier Sammut, Balzan; tel: 9944 9925; www.fragiuseppe.com; Tue–Sun 10.30am–2pm, 6.30pm–late; map p.135 D1

Previously the home of Rev Dr Giuseppe, a Maltese doctor, this restored 300-year-old townhouse rests in a sheltered corner away from the hustle and bustle of this pretty village. Look out for Latin wall inscriptions discovered in 1980 during the redecoration process, or just sit back in a truly Mediterranean environment sipping some wine or nibbling on the great bar snacks. We love the abundant meat and cheese platter.

Ta Marku Wine Bar

Ally 6, St Lucy's Street, Naxxar; tel: 2141 5889; times vary; map p.135 D2

Minutes' walk from Naxxar centre, keep your eyes peeled for signs directing you to this restaurant-cum-wine bar. Sample the excellent wine and shared platter nibbles prepared in a welcoming and family-run environment, and don't miss out on the Snickers cake, which is rather addictive. You can't help but feel at home here.

The Wine Theatre

1, Valley Road, Birkirkara; tel: 2148 8593; www.thewine theatre.com.mt; summer closed, open Tue–Sat 8.30pm–late; map p.135 D1

If you like what you see behind the glass café counters, why not take some home? Most cafés offer a takeaway service, and sweets, pastries, biscuits, pies and cakes can be boxed and taken home as an ideal gift. Do bear the heat of summer in mind – food spoils very quickly, and cream cakes do not travel well. Malta's famous bite-sized almond biscuits, on the other hand, are ideal.

With live music and over 100 fine wines to choose from, this really is a great little place worth discovering. Bear in mind that the entertainment is sometimes in Maltese and the food is rather pricey; but the atmosphere is fun.

Zmerc Pub
131, Bribal Street, Balzan; tel: 2144 4576; daily until late; map p.135 D1
This punchy little place, in the residential area of Attard, oozes character. Serving traditional Maltese food and free appetisers; the drinks are cheap and the mood eclectic.

BAHAR IC-CAGHAQ, BUGIBBA AND ST PAUL'S BAY

Rookies Sports Bar
Triq il-Sponoz, Bugibba; tel: 2757 4550; Mon–Fri 7pm–late; Sat– Sun noon–late; map p.134 C3
Enjoy the fun atmosphere offered by one of the island's best sports bars, which also plays great music and serves good

food. Head to the popular Battle of the Bands gig every Wed, which features the best local talent.

THE THREE CITIES

Del Borgo
Triq San Duminku, Birgu; tel: 2180 3710; daily 7pm–1am; map p.135 E1
Modern decor meets traditional in this restored 18th-century cellar. Peruse the 150-bottle wine list and enjoy a light bite at the comfortable tables.

Il-Forn Wine Bar
27, Triq il-Tramuntana, Birgu; tel: 2182 0379; Tue–Sun 7.30pm–1am; map p.135 E1
Situated in the medieval city of Vittoriosa, this place has a band of local loyal followers who love it. Get to grips with the extensive wine list and the Mediterranean nibbles, including antipasto platters, breads and dips.

Lupanara Wine Bistro
Seagate Vaults, Fort St Angelo, Birgu; tel: 7947 8971; www.lupanarabistro.com; daily with exceptions; map p.135 E1
This comfortable little gem hosts popular jazz nights, as well as last-Friday-of-the-month Flamenco events.

THE NORTH

D-Vine Lounge
262, Main Street, Mellieha; tel: 2152 4345; www.dvine lounge.com.mt; Mon–Sat 8pm–late; map p.134 B3
Mellieha's newest, chic-est haunt, just off the main road. A vibrant and comfortable interior makes for a romantic setting, and the bar snacks are great.

Left: *a great view over the harbour of Valletta.*

GOZO AND COMINO

Bo Jangles
St Paul's Square, Marsalforn, Gozo; tel: 2155 4646; www.bojanglesgozo.com; Mon closed, Tue–Fri 6pm–1am, Sat–Sun noon–late, closed 4–30 Jan; map p.138 C4
A traditional English pub with all the trimmings: old and new faces, families and young people are all welcome in this friendly venue. There's beer, deals at the bar, pub food and free Wifi.

CAFES

VALLETTA

Cafe Prego
58, South Street; tel: 2133 4062; Mon–Sat 7.30am–7pm; map p.132 A2
Here, the 1960s live on. This place opened back in 1947 and little has changed! A Valletta institution serving hot and cold drinks and good food.

Caffe Cordina
244/5 Republic Street; tel: 2123 4385; www.vol.net.mt/caffe cordina; Mon–Sat 8am–7.30pm, Sun 8am–2.30pm; map p.132 B2
One of the stalwarts of the Valletta café culture scene. Features a vaulted ceiling embellished with Giuseppe Cali's artwork, there's a lot of history here. The service sometimes leaves a lot to be desired, especially if you're sitting outside, and the prices are steep. Sit inside to soak up the decor and enjoy the vast range of Maltese sweets and pastries.
SEE ALSO FOOD AND DRINK, P.69

Fumia Cafe
Old Bakery Street; tel: 2131 7053; Tue–Sun 8.30am–8.30pm; map p.132 B2

Just off the Manoel Theatre; grab a coffee and a Sicilian treat in this fabulous, glass-roofed courtyard.

L-Ingliz Tea Room
19, St John's Street; tel: 2122 1482; www.lingliztearoommalta.com; Mon–Fri 8am–4pm, Sat 10.30am–4pm; map p.132 B2
Bringing Britain back, proprietor Janet Vella makes homemade scones and cakes that have garnered quite a reputation for themselves. Specialty teas are also available.

SLIEMA, ST JULIAN'S AND PACEVILLE

Answers
Wilga Street, Paceville; daily until late; map p.135 E2
A super spot for a quick treat. Answers is ideal for a holiday lunch, or afternoon tea, at reasonable prices. Bottomless coffee day is on Thursdays.

Busy Bee Café
7, Antonio Bosio Street, Ta Xbiex; tel: 2133 1738; www.busybee.com.mt; Tue–Sat 9am–10pm, Sun 8am–10pm; map p.135 E1
A Maltese institution, Busy

While most cafés offer free Wifi to paying customers, the number of internet cafés in Malta has dwindled. If you're laptop-free try **Ziffa Cafe** (194, Strait Street, Valletta; tel: 2122 4307; Mon–Sat 9am–11pm, Sun 10am–4pm; €3 for 35 minutes; map.132 C3), which has numerous PCs to choose from and offers printing, photocopying and CD-burning too.

Bee has been serving tea, coffee and cakes to the Maltese for as long as anyone can remember. Tea, coffee and a large selection of scrumptious cakes and ice cream; the team are famous for *kannoli* – pastries filled with ricotta, sugar, fruit and pieces of chocolate (only available in winter).
SEE ALSO FOOD AND DRINK, P.69

Cafe Giorgio
17, Tigne Seafront, Sliema; tel: 2134 2456; Apr–Oct 8am–midnight, Nov–Mar 8am–10pm; map p.135 E2
An elegant corner café with brass and wood interiors, this really is the place to see and be seen. Order a

coffee, tea, spirit or snack while watching the world go by. Prices can be steep.

Cara's Cafe
248, Tower Road, Sliema; tel: 2134 3432; daily 9am–1am; map p.135 E2
A blend of outdoor tables, the busy promenade atmosphere and an alluring fresh coffee aroma. Known for its exquisite cakes and pastries, as well as its savouries; free Wifi is available.

Offshore
4, The Strand, Sliema; daily 7.30am–11pm; map p.135 E2
Stop by after a morning of shopping and you'll fit right in with the young, hip crown who love this central Sliema haunt. The potato wedges and fresh smoothies are particularly popular.

Stella's Coffee Shop
Level 3, The Plaza, Bisazza Street, Sliema; tel: 2133 0205; Mon–Sat 9am–7pm; map p.135 E2
Family-run, this cosy coffee shop is far from what you'd expect of most mall

Right: Mdina's famous Fontanella. **Below:** café life in Gozo.

cafés. The food is great and the drinks are yummy; save room for a freshly prepared sweet or savoury crêpe.

MDINA, RABAT, DINGLI

Fontanella Tea Garden
1, Bastion Square, Mdina; tel: 2145 0208; June–Sept 10am–11pm, Oct–May 10am–6pm; map p.134 C1
Famous for its unobstructed views; try to bag a table on the bastions. Sit under the red and white umbrellas and devour a slice of Fontanella's famous chocolate cake.

THE CENTRE

B R Guest
Smart Shopping Complex, Naxxar Road, Birkirkara; tel: 2144 1122; Mon–Sat 7am–noon, Sun 8am–noon; map p.135 D1
Need a break from the city? Unwind with a drink and dine on mouth watering, freshly baked bread, *arancini* (rice balls) or a delicious Danish pastry.

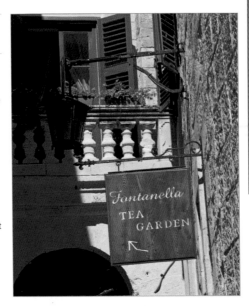

Café Luna
Palazzo Parisio, Victory Square, Naxxar; tel: 2141 2461; www.palazzoparisio.com; daily 9am–6pm; map p.135 D2
Probably the best tearoom on the island, this is a stylish daytime café in the heart of a magnificent palazzo. Get comfortable, you'll be staying a while.

GOZO

Cafe Royal
5, Independence Square, Victoria; tel: 9982 5783; daily 8am–noon; map p.138 B3
Serves coffee, tea and sandwiches opposite the flea market in Victoria. Try the delicious pizzas – they come highly recommended.

Beaches, Bays and Promenades

Unless you're staying in the north of Malta, it's unlikely you'll be within easy reach of a sandy beach. But don't despair, as the Maltese Islands offer numerous ideal spots for bathing and sun lounging, and swimming off the natural rocks is extremely popular. With the fantastic climate, beach life often lasts well into October, and there are plenty of water sports facilities. There are several appealing bays to explore, too, many of them surrounded by marinas and promenades with bobbing boats that make for pretty evening walks.

BEACHES AND BAYS

Malta has beaches to suit all tastes, from sunbathers to swimmers, sports enthusiasts and those with small children. Choose from golden sand, red sand, rocks, blue lagoons and even inland seas.

Anchor Bay

l/o Mellieha; daily 9.30am–5pm; bus: 44, 45; map p.134 A3
What was once a sleepy bay is now set within the bustling **Popeye Village Fun Park**. A great lido equipped with sun beds, umbrellas and ongoing activities for the children. Not a tranquil retreat, but plenty of fun for families.
SEE ALSO CHILDREN, P.42

Balluta Bay

St Julian's; bus: 62, 64, 65, 67, 68, 70, 627, 645, 652, 671; map p.135 E2
The stretch of coast that connects Sliema and St Julian's is dotted with swimming and sunbathing spots. The sea here is deep but generally clean, clear and safe to swim in.

Above: Golden Bay.

There are numerous lidos along the way.

Blue Lagoon

Comino; map p.139 E1
Dazzling blue waters off a tiny beach. Beautiful and worth the boat ride over from the mainland. Beware the throngs of day-trippers during the summer months and be prepared to jostle for a sun bed on the rocks.

Ghadira (Mellieha) Bay

Mellieha; bus: 44, 45, 48, 145; map p.134 B4
Also known as Mellieha Bay, this is Malta's

longest sandy beach, with plenty of space for lounging and activities. It does get quite crowded, but there is a good range of facilities on offer and shallow waters for paddling.
SEE ALSO CHILDREN, P.43

Ghajn Tuffieha

l/o Mellieha; bus: 47, 52, 652; map p.134 A2
One of the most unspoilt sandy beaches on the island, although families with young children are often put off by the trek down (and up) 180 stairs. Unmissable if you're looking for unspoilt views, especially at sunset.

Golden Bay

l/o Mellieha; bus: 47, 52, 652; map p.134 A2
Definitely one of the most popular beaches on the island, with lovely views and ample space. Surrounded by dramatic cliffs, access is easy and the waters generally safe, making it perfect for families with young children.

Left: Ramla Bay, Gozo.

ming. You will need to take a car or taxi to get here.

Paradise Bay
Marfa, Mellieha; bus: to nearby Cirkewwa 45, 48, 145, 167, 450, 645; map p.134 A4
Down a long flight of steps to a lido and sandy beach, this spot is remote and stunning, with views over to Gozo. The nearest bus stop is quite a walk away, so this is more ideal if you have a car.

Perched Beach
Dolmen Road, Bugibba; bus: 48, 49, 58, 59, 86; map p.134 C3
A new manmade stretch of sand has appeared below the promenade, creating a lovely, manicured sandy beach in the heart of this tourist district. A perfect mix of sand to lounge on and rocks to swim off. Accessible by wheelchair.

Pretty Bay
Birzebbugia; bus: 11, 12, 13, 113, 115; map p.137 D1
One of few beaches in the south of Malta, Pretty Bay is, as its name suggests, pretty – but the view of the nearby Freeport is not. If you don't mind that, this makes for a great sandy spot with plenty of space.

Water Sports
Malta is the perfect location for water sports – whether you are a professional or are hoping to try your hand at something for the first time. The follow sports are all widely practised, and you will find facilities for them at most beaches:
Sailing
Windsurfing
Diving
Canoeing
Kayaking
Jet-skiing and water-skiing
Kite-surfing and para-kiting

Little Armier Bay
Mellieha; bus: 50; map p.134 B4
On the northern tip of Malta, this is a getaway favoured by locals who don't mind that it's a little off the beaten track. Expect a small sandy beach well served by bars, restaurants and umbrellas. Perfect for paddling.

Right: popular, pebbly Mistra Bay is only accessible by car.

Mgarr ix-Xini
Gozo; map p.139 C1
In a gorge accessible from Xewkija and Sannat, this secluded spot is ideal for swimming and country walks, as well as being very attractive to divers. You'll need a car or boat to get to it, but the trek is certainly worth it.

Mistra Bay
Xemxija; map p.134 B3
Mistra Bay is a pebbly beach between Xemxija Bay and Selmun. The surrounding area is pretty, but the waters aren't always clean enough for swim-

Ramla Bay
Ramla, Gozo; bus: 42; map p.139 D3

Tourists and locals are drawn in by Ramla Bay's size and natural beauty. Popular thanks to its fiery red sand, great facilities and stunning views, no day in Gozo is complete without a trip and lounge here.

St George's Bay
St Julian's; bus: 66; map p.135 E2

St George's Bay was the first beach in Malta to undergo a replenishment programme, which completely transformed it. What was once a barren space overlooking the sea has been revamped to create a popular sandy beach, just a moment's walk from the island's entertainment district.

Xlendi Bay
Xlendi, Gozo; bus: 87; map p.138 A2

A perfect spot for families, this tiny bay blends paddling and swimming with charm and a typical Mediterranean lifestyle. Safe and surrounded by dramatic cliffs and little fish restaurants, there is plenty to do here during the summer months.

PROMENADES AND MARINAS
Boating is big in Malta, and as a result berthing space for yachts and cabin cruises is limited. The marinas that do exist are pretty and bursting at the seams – very enjoyable if you fancy life on the high seas, as this is the place to find inspiration for the boat of your choice. There are also numerous promenades to saunter along, all of them surrounded by spots to sit, drink, eat or grab an ice cream while soaking up the unbeatable aura of a Mediterranean evening.

The Ferries
Sliema; bus: 61, 63, 65, 70, 627, 645, 652; map p.135 E2

Definitely the most popular promenade, especially with locals who love

Boat Tours

Had enough of simply looking at the sea from a distance? Hop on one of the many boat trips available and you'll grow sea legs in no time!
Alliance Cruises, tel: 2133 2165, www.alliance cruises.com
Captain Morgan, tel: 2346 3333, www.captainmorgan.com.mt
Hera Cruises, tel: 2133 0583, www.herayachtmalta.com
Sundream Travel, tel: 2138 0133, www.sundreams travel.com

people-watching while on their evening walk. Nicknamed 'The Ferries' for obvious reasons (this is the kick-off point for the majority of the boat tours around Malta), you'll find outdoor cafés and restaurants here, as well as the odd souvenir shop that stays open into the evening.

Gzira Marina

Gzira; bus: 61, 63, 141, 627; map p.135 E2
Starting in Mdina and winding its way along to Ta Xbiex, the Gzira Promenade and marina make for an enjoyable walk overlooking the entrance to Valletta and Manoel Island. A flat stretch, dotted with ice-cream vans and snack spots, there is also a beautiful garden to walk through with swings and slides for the children. The yacht marina here is one of the largest and most established in Malta, while the adjacent Manoel Island (which is connected via a small bridge) houses a quaint duck island among other things.

Islet Promenade

Bugibba; bus: 48, 49, 58, 59, 86; map p.134 C3
Perfect for an evening stroll, especially if you're after something more upbeat. Islet Promenade stretches from Qawra to Bugibba in a seemingly endless curve around the coast, overlooking Comino and Gozo. Usually overrun with families, dog-walkers and joggers, there is something to keep most people happy – from ice-cream parlours to bumper cars and benches with a view to restaurants with a vista. Touristy, true, but perfect for whiling away summer evenings surrounded by a busy and fun-filled atmosphere.

Marsalforn

Gozo; bus: 21; map p.138 C4
Gozo is generally

Left: Pretty Bay is a great choice for families *(see p.37)*.
Right: Islet Promenade.

described as a tranquil haven that offers little to those holidaymakers seeking a vacation full of jam-packed action, but Marsalforn is full of life, especially during the summer. Admittedly small, it stretches from the Calypso Hotel complex, which boasts numerous seafront cafés and restaurants, to a large swing park and the island's famous saltpans. Bursting with Gozitan spirit, there is also a tiny sandy beach to paddle off.

Marsascala Bay

Marsascala; bus: 17, 19, 20, 22; map p.137 E2

If you're in the south, Marsascala Bay is one of the prettiest spots to visit, especially in the evenings. A short, fairy-lit promenade takes you around the coast, while little *luz-zus* (local, brightly coloured fishing boats) bob on the water. Soak up the atmosphere, and the view of the prominent parish church in the back-

ground, which can be enjoyed from iron benches dotted en route.

Portomaso Marina

Paceville, St Julian's; bus: 62, 64, 65, 66, 67, 68, 70, 627, 645, 652, 671; map p.135 E2

The first privately owned marina on the island, this is the berthing spot of choice for those for whom money is no object. Upmarket and exclusive, it makes for a beautiful and romantic walking spot just a moment's walk

from the centre of Paceville. Enjoy a stroll before drinking, or dining, in one of the marina's popular eateries.

Spinola Bay

St Julian's; bus: 62, 64, 65, 66, 67, 68, 70, 627, 645, 652, 671; map p.135 E2

Perfect for a romantic walk, Spinola Bay offers a bit of everything – including a massive marble statue spelling out the word LOVE. The fairy-lit bay is surrounded by some of the island's best upmarket eateries. The walk from Balluta Bay *(see p.36)* takes about 15 minutes, but if walking is not your thing, you could always take a gondola back.

Tower Road

Sliema; bus: 62, 63, 64, 65, 67, 68, 70, 645, 652, 671; map p.135 E2

Connecting Sliema to St

Left: ultra-posh Portomaso Marina. **Right:** Valletta Waterfront.

Left: the infamous LOVE bridge in Spinola Bay.
Right: Tower Road.

Julian's, this is a flat and manageable stretch enjoyed by cyclists, joggers and rollerbladers. Especially busy on summer evenings there is something to be enjoyed by everyone here, including a large swing park, ice-cream parlours, numerous restaurants and chic cocktail bars.

Valletta Waterfront

Valletta; bus: 198; map p.133 C1–E3

Not to be missed, this stunning waterfront promenade is a feather in the cap of those who undertook its renovation and completed it to the highest standards. What was once a derelict and forgotten piece of land (originally an 18th-century wharf), has been given a mammoth makeover, transforming it into a hotbed of activity both day and night. Enjoy a

stroll along the paved walkway, browse the upmarket souvenir shops or catch a bite in one of the many trustworthy eateries set within 19 250-year-old warehouses.

Vittoriosa Waterfront

Vittoriosa; bus: 1, 2, 300; map p.135 E1

A promenade oozing with history, stunning views across the Grand Harbour and plenty of atmosphere. Another recent renovation project has brought this spot into the new millennium and has developed it to become the home of several super-yachts (perfect for star gazing) and numerous great bars and restaurants. Worth the trek to this often overlooked part of the island.

Children

As a historical sun and sea destination, Malta has plenty to offer families with young children. Time on a sandy beach is well spent, as the majority of them have shallow areas, great for paddling. Little ones will also enjoy exploring the silent streets of Mdina as their imaginations run riot. The traditional orange buses, while not particularly punctual, can be great fun. Malta is popular as a safe destination, and parents can sit back and relax while the kids play nearby. The biggest worry is keeping them cool in the summer sun, a problem easily solved with generous helpings of gelato and sunscreen.

ANIMALS
Mediterraneo Marine Park
Coast Road, Bahar ic-Caghaq; tel: 2137 2218; www.mediter raneo.com.mt; daily 10am–5.45pm; map p.135 D3
Swim with dolphins or catch a sea lion or parrot show. Enjoy an experience that allows you to come up close and personal with some of nature's most amusing and amazing creatures.

ATTRACTIONS
Mdina Dungeons
St Publius Square, Mdina; tel: 2145 0267; www.dungeons malta.com; daily 9.30am–4pm; map p.134 C1
While younger children may be spooked, older ones will love discovering the torturous activities that

Lather your little ones in sunscreen when temperatures soar. The strong breeze by the sea can mask temperatures, but don't be fooled. It is advisable to keep light clothing on at all times, and a sun hat is a must.

once went on in this fortified city. Expect plenty of waxworks and ghoulish sound effects.

Playmobile Funpark & Factory
Hal-Far; tel: 2224 2445; www.playmobilemalta.com; Mon–Sat 10am–5.45pm, Sun 10am–1pm; map p.137 D1
Kids will love this indoor and outdoor play area. Plus there are animated activities on every day during the summer months and at weekends through the year.

Be the first to see and buy these well-known toys on the factory tour, before they are packed and sent to shops around the world.

Popeye Village
Anchor Bay, Mellieha: tel: 2152 4782; www.popeyemalta.com; daily 9.30am–5.30pm; map p.134 A3
This original film set has all the makings of a great day out. Step back in time to when a young Robin Williams starred as the iconic Popeye, slide into the splash pool, take a boat ride round the bay, play video games, join a mini-golf tournament or simply lounge on the private rocky beach.

SEE ALSO BEACHES, BAYS AND PROMENADES, P.36

Splash and Fun Water Park
Coast Road, Bahar ic-Caghaq; tel: 2137 4283; www.splashand fun.com.mt; daily 9am–9pm; map p.135 D3
Children of all ages will love zooming down the slides of Malta's only water

Left: Popeye Village reuses the set used for the Popeye film in 1980.

National Museum of Natural History

Vilhena Palace, St Publius Square, Mdina; tel: 2145 5951; www.heritagemalta.org; daily 9am–5pm; charge; map p.134 C1

Kids will love the large collection of 10,000 rocks and minerals, over 3,500 birds, birds' eggs and nests, 200 mammals, over 200 fish species and thousands of local and exotic shells and insects.
SEE ALSO MUSEUMS, P.86

park. Animators keep the whole family occupied, while highlights include the lazy river, wave pool and dinosaur park.

BEACHES
Ghadira (Mellieha) Bay

Mellieha; bus: 44, 45, 48, 145; map p.134 B4

A great sandy beach for families to splash around on together. This is the island's largest beach, and there are spots of shallow water, perfect for paddling. There is also a large, inflatable playground out at sea. Swim out to it or take a ride on a dinghy before trampolining or sliding into the water from a great height. This may not be suitable for younger children.
SEE ALSO BEACHES, P.36

MUSEUMS
Museum of Toys

10, Gnien Xibla Street, Xaghra, Gozo; tel: 2156 2489; Mon–Sat 10am–noon, 3–6pm with exceptions; map p.138 C3

A stunning private collection of toys dating back to the late 18th century. Young children will love exploring the toys of yesteryear, while the young at heart will relish the trip down memory lane.
SEE ALSO MUSEUMS, P.90

Maltese school children are on vacation from July to October, so expect all attractions to be much busier during this period. Booking is advisable for most activities, and check websites to see whether you can buy online to avoid disappointment.

Above left and right: Splash and Fun Water Park.

43

Churches

With more than one church for every day of the year, Malta is certainly the spot to come to for a religious vacation or one that needs a little divine inspiration. Aside from the country's cathedrals, each village centres around its parish church, and each vies in splendour with its neighbour, with decorated ceilings and lush drapery; some even house works of merit from local and foreign artists. The islands are also swarming with little wayside chapels, some of which have been around for centuries, braving the elements on cliff sides or by the sea.

VALLETTA

Our Lady of Mount Carmel

Old Theatre Street; tel: 2123 3808; daily 6am–7pm; map p.132 B3

Built during the 1500s, the beautiful church with its detailed interior is still a place for prayer and religious practice. Visit before preparations for Saturday night mass and see the friar dressed in his oldey-worldey brown garb.

Our Lady of Victory Church

Victory Square; tel: 2124 5680; daily 7am–noon, 5–7pm with exceptions; map p.132 B1

The first church built in Valletta and one that commemorated the islands' victory over the Turks during the 1565 Great Siege. Paintings include two stunning examples by Francesco Zahra and Ermenegildo Grech. Grand Master La Vallette was originally buried here.

St Barbara

Republic Street; tel: 2165 1057;

Above: St Paul's Anglican Cathedral.

Mon–Sat 10.30am–11.20pm, Sun 9am–1pm, 5–6.30pm; map p.132 B1

Step past the dilapidated exterior to absorb the beautiful altar inside. Fairly small and old yet still oozing character and charm, this is the place to hear mass in different languages, including English, German and Italian.

St John's Co-Cathedral

St John's Square; tel: 2122 0536; www.stjohnsco

cathedral.com; Mon–Fri 9.30am–4.30pm, Sat 9.30am–12.30pm; map p.132 B2

The island's pride and joy; it's easy to while away many hours looking at the incredibly ornate decor of this huge church. Home to a beautiful art collection, including Giuseppe Mazzuoli's marble statue of John the Baptist and Caravaggio's *The Beheading of St John*. Look down as you pad through the church and note that the terracotta and white marble chequerboard floor is actually a series of plaques remembering the dead.

SEE ALSO MUSEUMS, P.85

St Paul's Anglican Cathedral

Independence Square; tel: 2122 5714; www.anglican malta.org; daily 7am–noon, 5–7pm with exceptions; map p.132 B3

Serves the Church of England and Anglican community. Built in 1844, its impressive tower is a Valletta landmark.

the church is plainer than most, with beautiful Maltese stone work. Look out for the stunning selection of statues held in aloves above the seating area.

The Millennium Chapel
Church Street, Paceville; tel: 2133 4464; www.millennium chapel.org; daily 9am–2pm; map p.135 E2
A place of peaceful prayer amidst bustling Paceville. Instituted by Augustinian fathers, residents of Paceville since 1934, and built with donations from religious locals, the idea was to create a tranquil spot for quiet contemplation and prayer. A youth mass is held here on Saturday at 9pm.

Parish Church of the Sacred Heart
Church Street, Sliema; tel: 2131 3505; www.sacrocuorparish. org; Mon–Fri 6.45am–10.30am, 5.15–7.15pm; map p.135 E2
Built in 1872 by Valletta priest Paul Vella, the church became a parish church in 1918. It hosts its annual *festa* on the first Sunday in July to celebrate the parish's dedication to Our Lady of the Sacred Heart.

Lavishly dressed and decorated statues are prominent features in Maltese churches. These statues are mounted on pedestals with poles and then carried through the village during its *festa* or other religious occasions. *See picture above and Festas, p.64–7*

St Paul's Shipwreck Chapel
74, St Paul's Street; tel: 2123 6013; Mon–Sat 7am–noon, 4–6.30pm, Sun 7am–noon; map p.132 C2
A hidden gem, this chapel is simple in its design and very peaceful. This church was planned by renowned architect Geronimo Cassar and was completed in 1582.

SLIEMA, ST JULIAN'S, PACEVILLE
Holy Trinity Anglican Church
75, Rudolph Street, Sliema; tel: 2133 0575; daily 9am–5pm; map p.135 E2

Right: the impressive Parish Church of the Sacred Heart.

This 'English country church' is quiet and peaceful; the perfect spot for contemplation, reflective thoughts and prayer. The tranquil atmosphere is enveloped by the Victorian Gothic stone structure.

Jesus of Nazareth
The Strand, Sliema; tel: 2131 6191; daily 7am–noon, 5–7pm with exceptions; map p.135 E2
Built by Marchese Ermolao Zimmermann Barbaro Di San Giorgio, this church became a parish church in 1973. It was dedicated to Jesus of Nazareth on 2 July 1895. The interior of

Left: Church of Our Lady of Mount Carmel.

had only three altars, with today's side chapels and choir added later on.

MDINA, RABAT, DINGLI
Church of Our Lady of Mount Carmel
Carmelites Convent, Triq Ville-gaignon, Mdina; tel: 2145 4524; daily 7am–noon, 5–7pm with exceptions; map p.134 C1
Designed by Francesco Sammut during the 1600s, this church took 12 years to complete. Explore the fine interior of seven altars and Palladian plasters under a well-lit oval nave-cum-dome.

Metropolitan Cathedral of St Paul
4, St Paul Square, Mdina; tel: 2145 4136; Mon–Sat 9.30am–4.45pm, Sun 3–5pm; map p.134 C1
Built following the 1693 earthquake destruction of original 13th-century facade, famous local archi-tect Lorenzo Gafä created today's Baroque structure with magnificent dome towers. Its form is comple-mented by the piazza it stands on.
SEE ALSO MUSEUMS, P.86

St Agatha's Church
The Motherhouse, St Agatha's, Rabat; tel: 2145 9222; Mon–Fri 8.30am–5pm, Sat–Sun 8am–noon; map p.134 B1
Originally built in 1504 and partially demolished; a larger structure was ele-vated in 1670. The marble statue of St Agatha above the altar was added in 1894, while the bell tower and lateral rooms were built 1912–13.

Right: Mosta Dome.

St Julian's Parish Church
5, Lapsi Street, St Julian's; tel: 2138 0270; www.stjulians parish.net; Mon–Sat 8.15–10am, 7–7.45pm, Sun 8.15am–1pm; map p.135 D2
With records of St Julian's place of birth being France, Belgium and Italy, the story of St Julian is said to be purely legend-ary. However, this legend hails St Julian as creator of a pilgrims' hospital, grant-ing him the title of patron saint. Perched on St Julian's Hill, this church pays homage to him.

St Patrick's Church
St John Bosco Street, Sliema; tel: 2133 0238; www.salesians malta.org; Mon–Sat 7am–1pm, Sun 6–7pm; map p.135 E2
A Roman Catholic church where you can also hear mass in English, it has been giving liturgical and sacramental service since its opening in 1905. Head along to listen to the chil-dren's choir at mass on the third Sunday of the month.

Stella Maris
42, Annunciation Street, Sliema; tel: 2133 4941; Mon–Sat 6.45am–10am, 5.30–7pm, Sun 6.30am–1pm, 5.30–7.30pm; map p.135 E2
The foundation stone for this iconic building was laid in 1855, on land donated by the Cathedral Chapter. Dedicated to Our Lady Star of the Sea (Stella Maris), it

46

St Paul's Cathedral

St Paul's Square, Rabat; tel: 2145 4467; Sat–Sun 9.30am–11am; map p.134 C1
Dating back to 1372 and built to the left of St Paul's Grotto. The dedication to St Paul comes from the tradition that St Paul spent three months praying in the grotto beside the church.
SEE ALSO ARCHITECTURE, P.29

THE CENTRE

Church of the Assumption (Mosta Dome)

15, Church Street, Mosta; tel: 2143 3826; Mon–Sat 9.15am–11.45am, Mon–Fri 3–5pm; map p.135 C2
Rebuilt around the original 1830–60 by Maltese architect Giorgio de Vasse. A replica of the 200-kg (440-pound) German bomb that pierced the dome in 1942, and miraculously failed to explode, can be viewed in the sacristy. Look up to view one of the largest domes in the world.

Villagers are very loyal to their parishes, and it has long been the tradition to give generously in order to help with the ongoing beautification process of the church. Long-time rivalries still exist between parishes, and often act as an incentive for parishioners to give more towards the local feast, procession, band march or fireworks display.

Church of the Nativity of the Virgin Mary

Victory Square, Naxxar; tel: 2143 5376; www.naxxarparish.org; Sun–Fri 6am–6.30pm, Sat 5–6.30pm; map p.135 D2
A beautiful and lavish church, the cruciform shape of the facade and aisles seen today were rebuilt by Tumas Dingli early the 20th century.

Parish Church of the Annunciation

36, Triq Idmejda, Balzan; tel: 2144 8333; daily 7am–9.30am, 4.30–7.30pm; map p.135 D1
The architectural design of the Latin cross began in 1665, with the first foundation stone laid in 1669. Works inside include paintings by Giuseppe Calleja and Chev. Emvin Cremona, as well as a statue by Salvu Dimech.

Parish Church of the Transfiguration

47, Transfiguration Square, Lija; tel: 2144 2553; www.lija parish.com; Mon–Sat 6am–9am, 4.30–7pm, Sun 6.30am–noon, 4.30–6.30pm; map p.135 D2
Originally became a parish on 6 February 1594; the present church was built 100 years later and dedicated by Bishop Labini on 25 July 1782. Today it is a fine example of Baroque architecture and recent restoration works preserved the priceless art of local painter Cali, found on the church's ceiling.

St Joseph the Worker Church

Triq Bwieraq, Birkirkara; tel: 2144 5004; daily 7am–noon, 5–7pm with exceptions; map p.135 D1

Work started in 1965 and it was elevated to parish church status in 1973. Designed by Mortimer and Degiorgio, it features entrances from two streets and displays a titular processional wooden statue made in Bolzano, Italy.

BAHAR IC-CAGHAQ, BUGIBBA AND ST PAUL'S BAY

Our Lady of Sorrows Church

Tower Street, St Paul's Bay; tel: 2157 9266; daily 7am–7pm, 5–7pm with exceptions; map p.134 C3

The influx of tourists that transformed St Paul's Bay into a summer resort led Countess Anna Bugeja to order the building of this church to compensate for the summer crowds. Home to artworks by Giuseppe Cali.

Among the most prominent paintings embedded within Maltese culture are those of **Mattei Preti**. His finest work, the frescoes depicted at St John's Co-Cathedral, display features of Maltese history. Preti died in 1699 and is buried within the cathedral itself.

THE THREE CITIES

Church of the Immaculate Conception

65, Triq il-Genduz, Cospicua; tel: 2182 8413; daily 7am–9am, 4.30–6.30pm; map p.135 E1

Situated in the second of the Three Cities, this was the only church in the town to survive the World War II bombings. Originally built in 1584 and enlarged in 1637, a monument to those fallen in World War II lies below the facade.

Maria Bambina Basilica

27 St Lawrence Street, Senglea; tel: 2182 7203; Mon–Sun 9.15am–12pm, 4.30pm–5.30pm; map p.135 E1

This church has quite a history. Erected after the

Rright: Ta Pinu Shrine.

Great Siege, it was built to commemorate the spot where the fiercest battles were fought. Sadly, it was extensively demolished by bombs during fierce air raids in the Second World War but was rebuilt to its former glory between 1950–7. Today it is one of the most richly decorated churches on the island. While exploring, look out for the intricate marble and bronze canopy over the main altar; art collection; silk damask tapestries; crystal chandeliers; and the countless silver artefacts.

St Lawrence Church

91, St Lawrence Street, Vittoriosa; tel: 2182 7057; daily 9.15am–noon, 4.30–5.30pm; map p.135 E1

A magnificent 16th-century building encompassing a splendid altarpiece, *Martyrdom of St Lawrence*, by famous Italian artist Mattia Pretti.

SEE ALSO ARCHITECTURE, P.29

Built on the grounds of a Roman Temple between 1697–1711. The Baroque structural form of the Latin cross, created from local limestone, boasts a tall belfry with five bells and opposing traditional double belfries on the front. In 1739 clever interior paintings were added to give the impression of a dome.
SEE ALSO MUSEUMS, P.89

St Lawrence Church
40, Pjazza San Lawrenz, San Lawrenz; tel: 2155 6073; daily 7am–noon, 5–7pm with exceptions; map p.138 A3
Unusual and fascinating, the artist of the interior statue is unknown, but we do know that it was brought by Spanish seafarers before the Order of St John arrived in 1530. The church's silver plinth features four statues by Abram Gatt, representing four virtues: faith, hope, charity and purity.

Ta Pinu Shrine
1, Triq it-Trux, Gharb; tel: 2155 6129; daily 5am–noon, 6.45–7.30pm; map p.138 A3
Construction of this magnificent Romanesque structure occurred between 1920–32. On 22 June 1883, spinster Karmela Grima claimed to have heard the voice of Our Lady of Ta Pinu as she passed the chapel, and it later became a shrine in remembrance of this occasion. Definitely worth a visit, the shrine is now home to countless letters and memorabilia from believers thanking Our Lady for protecting them during times of need. Items include baby clothes, crutches and bandages.

THE SOUTH
Our Lady of Pompeii
39, Our Lady of Pompeii Square, Marsaxlokk; tel: 2165 0662; daily 5.30–8am, 4.30–7.30pm; map p.137 E2
Situated in Marsaxlokk, a local sacred spot in ancient times. Following Marsaxlokk's transformation into a summer resort, the church became a local parish in 1897. This is the venue of the annual national pilgrimage on 8 May.

St Anne's Church
Pjazza Dun Tarcis Agius, Marsascala; tel: 2163 3703; www.marsaskala-malta.com/parishchurch; daily 7am–noon, 5–7pm with exceptions; map p.137 E2
Built to serve the spiritual needs of summer residents and dedicated to the mother of the Virgin Mary. Don't miss the splendid marble altar and painting of St Anne hanging in the main vestry.

Left: St Lawrence Church, Vittoriosa.

THE NORTH
Nativity of the Virgin Mary Church
Parish Square, Mellieha; tel: 2152 3449; daily 7am–noon, 5–7pm with exceptions; map p.134 B3
Despite the fleeing from this locality, driven by fear of corsair raids during the war, the church remained a centre of devotion.

GOZO AND COMINO
Church of St Peter and St Paul
28th April Street, Nadur; tel: 2155 1649; www.nadurparish.com; daily 7am–noon, 5–7pm with exceptions; map p.139 D2
This parish devoutly remembers the sufferings of Apostles Peter and Paul. A myriad of artists have left their mark. Look to ceiling painting by Lizani Pisani, depicting moon and sun creations, and symbolising the two devoted Apostles.

Gozo Cathedral
Cathedral Square, Victoria; tel: 2155 4101; daily 7am–noon, 5–7pm; map p.138 B2

Cultural Activities

Culture on the Maltese Islands bubbles through every part of life, and passion is the undertone of every activity. The majority of the cultural calendar revolves around religion, and the country comes alive over the Christmas period and again for the more sombre Easter rituals. While government funding is, as a rule, still lacking for the arts, a growing scene is evident, and most weekends you can catch an English-language play, art exhibition or dance performance in one of the islands' numerous performance spaces. Meanwhile, the local music scene becomes more adventurous each year so, be sure to catch a live gig if you can find one.

RELIGIOUS ACTIVITIES

ADVENT AND CHRISTMAS

Christmas is a great time to visit Malta, as the weather usually remains mild, while the country comes alive to the sound of carols playing through the streets, endless celebratory activities and an overall sense of celebration.

Here Christmas is a very religious holiday, and while the unavoidable commercial aspect creeps in more and more each year, the birth of Jesus remains at the core of all the festivities. In fact, most houses and shops will display a nativity crib (or *presepju*) with decorated figurines representing Joseph, Mary, baby Jesus, shepherds, villagers and animals surrounded by flowers and plants. Live nativities, performed through the village streets, are also gaining popularity and are great fun if you can make it to one.

Above: the fabulous Astra Theatre in Gozo.

At the centre of the celebrations is each parish church, which is decorated with lights, flowers and nativity cribs for the occasion. On Christmas Eve most villagers take to the streets for a procession, followed by midnight mass, which is a tradition that is still going strong. Midnight mass includes a sermon given by a young boy chosen from the parish. In true Mediterranean style, most families flock to an early-bird Christmas breakfast straight after mass, before heading home to get the joyous Christmas celebrations into full

Theatre in Malta
You may be surprised by the fantastic level of theatre on show in Malta. The vibrant scene, which sees full-scale productions go on almost every weekend during the October–July season, is produced by 'amateurs' – but only because there will never be the volume to support a professional industry. The Malta Amateur Dramatics Club (MADC) turned 100 in 2010, celebrating its amazing history since it was first launched by British expats. If you can catch one of their shows (e.g. the hilarious Christmas pantomime held at the MFCC, Ta Qali), or indeed any of the many English-language productions held, you'll be in for a treat.

Right: the Aurora Opera House in Gozo, *(see p.52)*.

Left: art festival in Gozo.

depicting the last hours of Christ's life are carried around the town and accompanied by the village band.

Easter day is traditionally celebrated with a family lunch, and it is customary to visit relatives and friends. It's also tradition to give children a *figolla* (an almond-filled pastry, covered in colourful icing) and Easter eggs.

VILLAGE FESTAS

Throughout summer, fireworks bang in the sky and villagers take to the streets to revel in annual celebrations dedicated to their patron saints. Examples of true Mediterranean spirit, dedication and passion, these feasts are not to be missed.

SEE ALSO FESTAS, P.64–7

THEATRES, GALLERIES AND LIVE MUSIC VENUES

Astra Theatre

9, Republic Street, Victoria, Gozo; tel: 2155 6256; map

swing with plenty of music and eating.

EASTER

The Maltese Islands take the feast of Easter extremely seriously, and religious activities are ongoing throughout this period.

Easter Sunday is actually the end of the Easter celebrations, which kick off with Ash Wednesday marking the beginning of Lent. Lent is a period of sacrifice, and those choosing to honour it will give up sweets and meat until the holy period is over.

Holy Week is packed with events, including the seven visits on Maundy Thursday and culminating in a unique and fascinating Good Friday procession. During the procession several life-sized statues

Above: one of Malta's best live music venues.

p.138 B3

A popular opera venue, the Astra Theatre is one of Gozo's two main theatres, and it boasts a somewhat surprising portfolio of world-renowned stars and shows. Inaugurated in 1968, there's a lot of history to be felt here, and it's worth trying to get tickets if there's something on.

Aurora Opera House
Republic Street, Victoria, Gozo; tel: 2156 2974; map p.138 B3
Renowned for its excellent operas, musical events, stage shows and ballets, this 1,600-seat theatre is one of the largest on the Maltese Islands.

BJ's
Ball Street, Paceville; tel: 2133 7642; daily from 10pm; map p.135 E2
One of the island's only established live music venues, BJ's is a blink-and-you'll-miss-it sort of place tucked down a Paceville side street. Best known for its annual Music Marathon, which raises money for worthy causes, BJ's offers daily sets from local and international musicians, as well as impromptu jam sessions and open-mic nights.

City Theatre
Old Bakery Street, Valletta; www.citytheatremalta.com; tel: 2180 8080; map p.132 A2
The newest of Valletta's theatre spaces, this good-sized venue was taken over in 2008 by one of the leading local theatre companies. Focusing mostly on Maltese-language productions, they are also known for importing foreign productions for children.

Malta Fairs & Conventions Centre
Millennium Stand Level 1, National Stadium, Ta Qali; tel: 2141 0371; www.mfcc.com.mt; map p.134 C1
Malta's largest international conference and exhibition venue, this recent addition to the scene has already become a hotspot for some of the biggest events and festivals on the island, including top international DJs, theatre, pantomimes, exhibitions and fairs. Check the website for updated listings.

Manoel Theatre
115, Theatre Street, Valletta; tel: 2122 2618; www.teatru manoel.com.mt; map p.132 C3
Definitely worth a visit if there's something on, this is Malta's national theatre and its pride and joy. Majestic and plush, it is reputed to be Europe's

> **Nadur Carnival**
> Forget the glitter of the traditional Carnival, the 'spontaneous' Nadur Carnival – held while the rest of the country watches the float parades in the bigger towns – is notable for its darker and more risqué themes. It is loud, uncomfortable and not for the children – but it is hilarious. Instead of fairies and princesses, spot cross-dressers, frightening masks and original ideas that all add to the eclectic party atmosphere.

third-oldest working theatre. One of the highlights is its three tiers of boxes constructed entirely of wood and decorated with 22-carat gold leaf, and a pale blue ceiling that resembles a round cupola. The theatre often hosts local and international performances covering opera,

drama and music as well as an unmissable Christmas pantomime.
SEE ALSO MUEUMS, P.84

MCA
8, Off Racecourse Street, Marsa; tel: 2122 6414; by appointment; map p.135 E1
Malta's only specialised contemporary art space opened in 2008 and is managed by the same artists who felt such a space was desperately needed. Set in a refurbished warehouse, recent works have proved popular and are helping to secure Malta's reputation on the international scene.

Mediterranean Conference Centre
Valletta; tel: 2124 3840; www.mcc.com.mt; map p.133 D3
Blending history with a modern theatre and conference space, the MCC is best known for the largest musicals and dance shows, but was once the hospital used by the Knights of St John.

MITP
St Christopher's Street, Valletta; map p.133 D2
Mostly managed by St James Cavalier, this city venue has gained popularity as an informal space for theatre, exhibitions and performance art. The venue of choice for alternative artists, this is where to catch Malta's emerging talent.

St James Cavalier Centre for Creativity
Castille Place, Valletta; tel: 2122 3216; www.sjcav.org; map p.132 B1
This is Malta's primary exhibition and performance space. The building itself, built by the Knights of St John, is splendid, and its regeneration has expertly blended old with new. Today it is alive with art of all kinds, from art exhibitions in the main hall and art-house films in the dinky cinema to concerts in the music room. An intimate 120-seat theatre space has now become one of the most popular performance venues on the island and often plays host to the best local and foreign talent. See the website for updated listings.

The Wine Theatre
1, Valley Road, Birkirkara; tel: 2148 8593; www.thewine theatre.com.mt; Tue–Sat winter only; map p.135 D1
A great little addition to the local scene, the Wine Theatre is exactly what it says on the tin – a wine bar and a theatre. With a weekly schedule that includes stand-up (usually

Music in Malta

Malta has an enthusiastic music scene, with fresh bands emerging onto the scene every few weeks merging an interesting mix of traditional, imported and experimental sounds. The most traditional form of local music is the *Ghana* – chanted poetry. The locals also love the Eurovision Song Contest and have kept their fingers and toes crossed every year since the competition began. Sadly, they have yet to win, but if you're here over Eurovision weekend, be sure to join in one of the merry parties held in bars across the islands. Meanwhile, Malta has also become a prime location for jazz through the Malta Jazz Festival, which is held annually towards the end of July.

Cultural Activities

53

Left: the St James Cavalier Centre for Creativity.

in Maltese), jazz and other live performances with great bar food and a fabulous wine list, you'll be laughing.

ANNUAL EVENTS

CARNIVAL

Held on the February weekend before Ash Wednesday (and as a last-minute celebration before the start of Lent), the flamboyant local Carnival has had an important place on the Maltese cultural calendar for just under five centuries, having been introduced to the Islands by Grand Master Piero de Ponte in 1535.

This is largely an event aimed at children, although most locals join in by donning some kind of colourful costume or other. The majority of the celebrations centre around Valletta and Floriana, where a massive

float procession makes its way through the streets. These huge floats, which are brightly coloured and made from papier-mâché, compete for the King Carnival crown while costume-bedecked dancers and singers perform in the main square.

Being Mala there had to be a local dish dedicated to the Carnival! The popular *prinjolata* is an enormous white dome of sponge made from seeds, almonds and eggs, coated with beaten meringue and chocolate, and topped with cherries. Not to be missed if you can find it!

THE GOZO MUSIC FESTIVAL

Gozo may be regarded as

Malta's sleepier sister, but not on the night of its music festival. Combining live local and international music acts as well as world-renowned DJs, it rocks Gozo for one August night every year. For this year's line up visit www.gozo musicfestival.com.

THE MALTA ARTS FESTIVAL

Now an annual event usually held in July, the Malta Arts Festival is gaining a reputation as one of the leading arts festivals in the Mediterranean. Combining local and international theatre, jazz, dance, exhibitions and live art, it may lack the vibrancy of other larger festivals on the continent but is certainly a step in the right direction.

Left: Malta's extravagant Carnival. **Right:** scene from the Malta Arts Festival. **Far Right:** the Gozo Music Festival

Diving

With their crystal clear waters and vibrant under-the-sea sights, it's no wonder the Maltese Islands were recently voted one of the top three dive destinations in the world. The vast number of dive schools in the vicinity make it a superb spot for beginners keen to test their fins, while more experienced seadogs will be fascinated by the historical wrecks and underwater scenery. Plus, the mild water temperatures (usually between 15°C/59°F and 27°C/80°F) mean it's never the wrong time to grab your aqualungs and jump in.

TOP DIVE SITES

The Maltese Islands' numerous dive sites are a concoction of wreckages, small reefs and pretty caves accessible by shore or boat. There are umpteen possible sites to choose from, but the following six offer guaranteed fun, adventure and incredible scenery.

CIRKEWWA

Locals love this dive, and for good reason. Reaching a maximum depth of 36m (118ft), it takes you through a number of caves and a dramatic arch that actually forms part of a cavern with a hole at the top. Other top attractions include the sunken tugboat *Rozi*, stunning caves, spectacular walls and the famed statue of the Madonna. Often calm, watch out for northwesterly winds which create tough diving conditions here.

COMINO

Located on the north side

Above: local companies are of the highest standard and know the best sites and wrecks like the back of their hand.

of Comino, Malta's tiny sister island, the Santa Marija caves are some of the most fascinating in the world. There are 10, each with its own highlight, ranging from breathtaking views into the blue to delightful inhabitants including octopuses, eels, mullets and lobsters. As if that wasn't enough, the beautiful setting was also featured in the blockbuster film *The Count of Monte Kristo*.

DWEJRA POINT, GOZO

With an impressive maximum depth of 60m (197ft) there is no debating the magnificence of this site. Colourful marine life is in abundance here, and the depth provides plenty of nooks and caves to explore through the crystal-clear waters. Travel through the Inland Sea and look out for the incredible underwater sights near Crocodile Rock, as well as the vibrant coral.

GHAR LAPSI, QRENDI

Minutes from this tiny fishing village in the south of Malta, this is a nice and straightforward dive, suitable for beginners. Depths usually range from 15 to 20m (50 to 65ft). Especially spectacular during the day, one of the highlights is a swim through a cave that has light streaming into it at the end. A great dive if you enjoy exploring caves.

Right: cave diving is very popular in Malta.

Left: resurfacing after an adventurous dive.

huge sunken tanker just a short swim from shore. Sadly, the wreck is the result of a tragic explosion in 1995 which killed nine local dockyard workers. In 1998 it was sent to its final resting place in the village of Zurrieq, close to the famed Blue Grotto. Look out for stunning sea life.

DIVE SCHOOLS

Local dive schools are experienced and knowledgeable, offering courses for beginners right up to technical qualifications. Even if you aren't looking to join a programme, it is still a good idea to contact them for advice on which dive sites best suit your abilities.

Aquaventure Ltd

The Waters Edge, Mellieha Bay Hotel, Mellieha; tel: 2152 2141; www.aquaventuremalta.com; map p.134 B3

One of the large local schools, Aquaventure has been in the business of taking people under the sea for years. With a wide range of PADI courses on offer, they are also known

---

Le Polynesian

Malta's version of the Titanic, *Le Polynesian* is a 19th-century passenger liner that was sunk by a German U-Boat at the end of World War One. The 152-m (500-ft) ship made her maiden voyage from France to Australia in 1891. The ship continued to make this journey, and others, until 1914 when it was hit by a torpedo and sank just outside Valletta's Grand Harbour.

LE POLYNESIEN

Also in the south of Malta, this is the islands' version of the *Titanic* – a 19th-century passenger liner sunk during World War II. Only suitable for very experienced and technical divers, it is great fun to explore. It lies upright on the seabed at a depth of 70m (230ft). Many artefacts remain intact, so there is great scope for exploration, but it is certainly advisable to ask a guide to accompany you.

UM EL FAROUD, ZURRIEQ

An unmissable experience for accomplished divers, the *Um El Faroud* is absolutely spectacular – a

Left: many of Malta's best sites are only accessible to divers, but snorkelling near the coast brings ample rewards, especially at the Blue Lagoon *(see p.36)*.

for their flexibility, and can often fit in last-minute requests at only a couple of days' notice. Teaching material is available in most European languages.

Um El Faroud
One of the most tragic incidents of Malta's naval history, the *Um El Faroud* was a Libyan tanker stationed for repairs in Malta for three years. An accidental gas explosion caused the ship to explode, killing the nine local dockyard workers on board. Following the explosion, the ship's doors were removed and it was later sunk close to the Blue Grotto. A plaque stands in memory of the men.

Atlantis Diving Centre
Qolla Street, Marsalforn Bay, Gozo; tel: 2155 4685; www. atlantisgozo.com; map p.138 C4
Based in Gozo this respected school offers everything from PADI beginners' courses to exciting night dives. That aside, they also have a well-stocked shop, equipment rental and services, accommodation services and airport transfers.

Calypso Diving Centre
The Seafront, Marsalforn, Gozo; tel: 2156 2000; www.calypso divers.com; map p.138 C4
Friendly and experienced staff will make you feel at ease from day one. They know their stuff, having been in the business since 1985, and as well as offering PADI courses are the only recognised BSAC school in Gozo.

Diveshack Scuba School
14a Qui Si Sana Seafront, Sliema; tel: 2133 8558; www. divemalta.com; map p.135 E2
Centrally located in the heart of Sliema, this school is open seven days a week, all year round. PADI professional instructors take both beginners and

experienced divers through their paces, and they also offer a course for professionals.

Dive Systems

Tower Road, Exiles, Sliema; tel: 2131 9123; www.divesystems malta.com; map p.135 E2
One of the most reputable schools on the island, Dive Systems has been open since the 1970s. A laid-back atmosphere and fantastic views across St Julian's Bay are all part of the service, and staff mingle with students on fun activities including BBQs and night boat trips; perfect if you are looking for a more relaxed and social approach.

Maltaqua

Mosta Road, St Paul's Bay; tel: 2157 1873; www.maltaqua. com; map p.134 C3
This dive school has pretty much led the way for decades and still stands as one of the best.

A great range of courses and staff who put safety and service first. They were recently awarded the BSAC School of Excellence status, one of only four schools outside of the UK.

Above: Gozo's Azure Window *(see p.23)*. **Right and left:** two important wrecks, *Le Polynesian* and *Um El Faroud*, can be accessed from Malta *(see p.56, 58)*.

Environment

As one of the most densely populated countries in the world, the Maltese Islands are home to 1,265 inhabitants per sq km (there are 32 per sq km in the US). Naturally this has knock-on effects, making agricultural land limited and increasing congestion, especially in the built-up towns and cities where greenery and open space is scarce. Pollution is another problem, and other issues include inadequate water supply, deforestation and the preservation of wildlife. But things are looking up, and the government, backed by the population, is now extremely focused on flexing its green fingers.

RENEWABLE RESOURCES

The islands have long felt the power struggle between its limited space and its burgeoning population and popularity, as the old-school power stations struggle to cope with the demand. With over 1 million tourists per year (on top of the 400,000 permanent residents), resources are well and truly dwindling, especially during the summer months. Air-conditioning and an increased need for electricity has stretched the grid to breaking point, and power cuts are not unusual.

Looking skywards to the sun seems obvious, especially in a country where the sun shines for most of the year. So, locals are turning to solar power, and €2 million worth of government incentives are helping buyers make the switch. Wind energy and hydropower are both also being considered as viable options for the future.

THAT'S RUBBISH

For years, the Maghtab dump (still visible from the coast) was the butt of most jokes – this growing landfill offered the only solution to a very smelly problem. Now that it's been closed, the focus has turned to recycling, and incentives have been put in place to encourage people. In fact, a separate truck now collects recyclable rubbish from people's doorsteps once a week, putting Malta in step with most other EU countries.

CONGESTION AND TRANSPORTATION

With more than 300,000 cars on Malta's roads congestion is a problem,

Left: this power plant may enjoy a great view, but Malta is beginning to harness the natural forces of sun and sea to power the island.

Left: traffic congestion on Malta's smaller roads is the most problematic environmental issue tourists will encounter.

Vision for Valletta, which was launched in 2009, includes more congestion-bashing ideas for the capital, and it's possible vehicles will be banned from the city completely.

FEELING HOT AND COLD

There's no doubt that the weather is changing. Summer arrives later than it used to but hangs around for longer, with temperatures soaring way past 40°C (104°F); winter is fiercer, with sharp, icy winds and damaging hailstones. While the Maltese Islands have never really known dangerously harsh weather conditions, it seems climate change could soon put a stop to that.

especially in towns. And once you've arrived in the city centre, parking is just as difficult to find as free-moving traffic.

We recommend that you avoid car travel in town, using it only for trips around the island – not just for the good of the environment, but also for your own sanity.

Valletta recently took a leaf out of the books of several European cities and imposed a congestion charge on those parking in the city, encouraging drivers to use the nearby Park & Ride facilities. The 2015

Bird-Hunting

Nicknamed the 'annual massacre' by those against it, and a 'God-given right' by those who are for it, bird-hunting remains an issue high on the national agenda. Activists long argued that Maltese hunters were wreacking havoc on the world's birdlife, as species, some of them endangered, were being shot down during their migration, thus affecting their breeding. Today, spring hunting has been banned by the EU and further restrictions have been put in place. Since the ban, significant improvements have been made, and the majority of hunters have upheld the law, helping partially to pacify this potentially contentious issue.

Essentials

W hether it's Malta's laid-back lifestyle or the English-speaking population, tourists often remark how at home they feel on the Maltese Islands. Getting to Malta is much like getting to anywhere in Europe, but while sea links do exist, most tourists arrive through the international airport in Luqa. Life here is modern, and communication to the rest of the world runs like clockwork – you are never far from a public phone, internet access or a post office, and the islands also boast excellent health-care facilities. The following listings are a rundown of information that may prove essential during your stay here.

CLIMATE
Malta has a typically Mediterranean climate with hot dry summers and generally mild winters. The temperature averages 14°C (57°F) in winter (November to April) and 32°C (90°F) in summer (May to October).The hottest hours of the day are between 11am and 4pm. The hottest period is July–September, during which protection from the sun should be worn at all times to avoid heatstroke or sunburn.

CUSTOMS AND VISAS
Passengers travelling from outside the EU will be required to pass through the 'Green' or 'Red' channels stating whether they have anything to declare. Most food items, obscene literature, films or books, counterfeit items and other such products are prohibited, and you will be required to declare them on entry.
　　EU nationals, as well as those from Australia, Canada and New Zealand,

do not require a visa. For updated information on countries requiring a visa to enter Malta visit: www.mfa.gov.mt.

EMBASSIES
Australia
Ta' Xbiex Terrace, Ta' Xbiex; tel: 2133 8201; www.embassy.gov. au/mt.html; map p.135 E1
United Kingdom
Whitehall Mansions, Ta' Xbien Seafront, Ta' Xbiex; tel: 2323 0000; www.britishhighcommis sion.gov.uk/malta; map p.135 E1
USA
Development House, 3rd floor, St Anne Street, Floriana; tel: 2561 4000; www.usembassy. state.gov; map p.135 E1

EMERGENCIES
Wherever you are on the Maltese Islands, if you need emergency assistance from the fire brigade, ambulance or police, call 112.

GAY AND LESBIAN
Despite its status as a predominantly Catholic country Malta has a bubbling gay and lesbian scene, but one which remains discreet. The

country celebrated its first gay pride parade in 1996, and while the political parties have all expressed support against homophobia and discrimination there has been no real progress on these issues yet.

LOCAL MEDIA
The national English-language newspaper *The Times* is available daily, as is the *Malta Independent*. Malta's only tabloid, *Malta Today*, is available on Wednesdays and Sundays.
　　Malta has three main TV stations. TVM is the national channel, and content here is usually in Maltese and largely conservative. The other two stations, NET and ONE, are linked to the main political parties.

MEDICAL ATTENTION
Health care in Malta is renowned to be among the best in the region. It is free to anyone with a European Health Insurance Card,

Right: keeping time at St John's Co-Cathedral in Valetta.

Left: the British legacy can still be found.

3.45pm and mornings only on Saturdays.

Most public telephones in Malta are card-operated (cards can be bought from souvenir and stationery shops).

Most mobile phones will function perfectly in Malta.

The area code for Malta is +356 and there are no regional codes.

TIME ZONE
GMT + 1 (GMT + 2 from the last Sunday in March to the last Sunday in October).

TIPPING
Tipping is not obligatory but can be added. The norm is around 10 percent of the final bill.

> A ban on **smoking** in all public places has been in effect since 2004, but many argue its effectiveness. It's not uncommon to spot smokers lighting up in pubs, bars and clubs. It is, however, important to bear in mind that a fine can be imposed if you're caught.

while agreements with other countries have also been made. If you are taken ill during your time here, contact or visit the nearest polyclinic to consult the doctor on duty. Polyclinics are found in Mosta, Bormla, Floriana, Gzira, Qormi, Rabat and Paola, and they fall under the free public health system.

Hospitals in Malta
Mater Dei, Msida (public health); tel: 2545 0000; map p.135 D1
St Philip's Hospital, Sta Venera (private); tel: 9967 6000; map p.135 D1

St James Hospital, Sliema (private); tel: 2133 5235; map p.135 E2

MONEY
The local currency is the euro. For the latest rates visit an exchange bureau or www.xe.com.

POST & TELEPHONES
Most towns will have branch post offices (Mon–Sat 7.30am–12.45pm), while the main Valletta branch (Car I-Annona, Castille Place) opens Mon–Fri 8.15am–

Festas

Every town or village in Malta and Gozo has at least one *festa* which it celebrates annually. Some are better known than others, with particular characteristics that have lived on for centuries, including auctions to win the prized role of carrying the statue through the village streets. These vibrant feasts are typical of the local passion and spirit, and everything from the facade of the church to the streetlamps comes alive with fairy lights and bunting for the occasion. Revellers take to the streets for a week of celebration, combining religious dedication with a non-stop party for all ages to enjoy.

HISTORY

There's long been speculation as to exactly where *festas* came from, but the likely story is that they were the result of a fusion of existing traditions which merged throughout the 19th century. Before that they were only tiny affairs, characterised by the distribution of bread, cakes, almonds, wine and fruit for those attending religious ceremonies, while the poor were also given money and food as a sign of good will.

It wasn't long before the more gaudy and bright aspects of these feasts trickled in. Illuminations by firewood or lamps provided some sparkle and, as early as 1738, mortars set off in Birkirkara to celebrate St Helen – a prequel to the full-blown fireworks displays of today.

FESTAS TODAY

The season lasts from around May to September, with the odd one held in the winter too (weather permitting). If you're here

Above: *festa* in Sliema.

over the summer you will be spoilt for choice, with around three to four *festas* happening concurrently in different villages around the islands.

Expect a complete transformation, and one that is taken very seriously by the villagers. Streets are adorned with flowers, flags, statues and lights, and lavishly decorated cloth banners are hung from one side of the road to the other. Activity is everywhere and ongoing

despite the inevitable heat, as children run around, stalls are set up selling their wares and the village band plays on.

While festivities carry on for a week, the actual feast day is what it's all about. The Maltese thank their village's patron saint zealously – there is much pealing of bells, noisy petards and splendid fireworks. This is the day to visit the parish church, as it will be decked out to the

Right: St Joseph *festa* in Birkirkara.

Left: bands, fairy lights and crowds come out for festas.

Despite their hospitable nature, the Maltese are generally private people, living behind closed doors. But *festa* time is enough to bring anyone out of their shell, and part of the process includes giving homes a good spring clean in order to open them up to their neighbours come the big day. While walking through the streets, take an opportunity to glance inside these neat houses to see how even individual homes are transformed with decorations, lights and religious ornaments for feast day – you may even get invited in!

nines in rich damasks, covered in flowers and smelling of incense.

The fireworks displays, the culmination of a year's work, are worth waiting for. Some argue that they are some of the most impressive in the world, and bright flashes light up the sky as each village tries to outdo its neighbour.

JOIN IN

No fewer than 90 feasts are celebrated through the year, with more than half of them dedicated to Our Lady. Each is a unique insight into traditional Maltese life, and you'll enjoy the experience whichever one you go to; visitors are always welcome. Some feasts have retained their particular characteristics.

For instance, the parish of St Helen in Birkirkara remains the only one to brave the August sun by holding its procession in the morning, while in St Julian's hunters on the roof of the church fire a salute as the procession comes out of the church.

Assumption of Our Lady

Mosta; 15 Aug; tel: 2143 3826; map p.135 C2

If you happen to be here for 15 August you'll be spoilt for choice for feasts to attend, with no fewer than seven parishes to choose from, all celebrat-

Above and below right: *festa* processions in Sliema.

Right: St Joseph *festa* in Birkirkara.

ing the Assumption of Our Lady. Mosta is one of the largest and most important feasts, and celebrations are held just outside this massive church. The fireworks display is impressive, lighting up the sky over Mosta's iconic dome.
SEE ALSO CHURCHES, P.47

Assumption of Our Lady
Mqabba; around 21 June; tel: 2164 9306; map p.137 E2

This tiny village in the south (not far from the airport) truly comes alive for its *festa*, and it's worth the trek to get here. Ground and aerial fireworks displays are held every day of the feast, organised by the award-winning Lily Fireworks Merlin Fire.

St Lawrence
Vittoriosa; 10 Aug; tel: 2182 7057; map p.135 E1
The patron saint of libraries and librarians, St Lawrence is the beloved patron of this seaside town

and they certainly know how to show him a good time. Never mind the small size of this village, its feast has grown to become one of the largest on the island, and the committee stop at nothing to raise funds for ever more exciting events year on year.
SEE ALSO CHURCHES, P.48

St Paul
Mdina; around 29 June; tel: 2145 6620; map p.134 C1
The silent city wakes up for its feast, and it's wonderful to watch one of Malta's greatest cathedrals done up for the occasion. The decorations inside are some of the best on the island. Events to look out for include the Procession with the Relics of the Saints from the Benedictine Church, and the Pontifical Concelebration

usually led by the arch-
bishop.
SEE ALSO CHURCHES, P.46

St Publius
Floriana; around 26 Apr;
tel: 2124 7106; map p.135 E1
Renowned for its impres-
sive fireworks display, this
is one of the earliest
feasts of the year. Take
the time to leave the rev-
elry outside and to visit
the church, which is lav-
ishly decorated in bright
red and gold, and
includes the prized silver
statue of St Publius.

St Sebastian
Qormi; 19 July; tel: 2148 6350;

map p.135 D1
Qormi is one of the most
traditional towns in Malta
and is worth a visit any-
way. Its *festa* is a time of
sheer jubilation, honour-
ing the parish of St
Sebastian, which was

created in 1936 as a sub-
sidiary of the main
church. St Sebastian
Band, founded in 1862
and the earliest of the
island's band clubs,
provides unabashed
entertainment.

Left: nougat and other treats
for sale during a *festa*.

Food and Drink

From freshly pressed olive oil to delicious crusty bread, the taste of the Mediterranean rings true in Malta and the locals love their food; you are never far away from a scrumptious and traditional snack here. The islands' eclectic historical background has added plenty of flavour to the array of dishes on offer. Speciality stores, including cafés and traditional confectioners, are the best places to sample traditional pastries and sweet treats, while hole-in-the-wall bakeries and *pastizzerijas* are unbeatable for savoury snacks including local pies and breads. *See also Wine, p.128.*

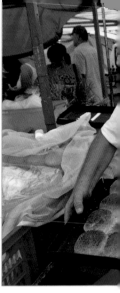

Left: *pastizzi* fresh from the oven.

them all down with a cold glass of local soft drink Kinnie or a pint of Cisk lager.

SAVOURY SNACKS AND DRINKS

If you want genuine and traditional fare, keep your eyes peeled for locals – they know where to look for the freshest and tastiest ingredients. Often off the beaten track, look out for the sight of a traditional bakery. Maltese bread *(hobz Malti)* is arguably one of the best in the world, with its thick crust and oozing white centre. Not great for the waistline, it is very moreish, especially when eaten hot out of the oven, dipped in olive oil and served with *gbejniet*, cheeselets made from goat's milk.

Another delectable delight is the famed *pastizzi*, a small pie made from light layers of filo pastry and stuffed with a pea or ricotta cheese mixture. Locals love them, and tiny *pastizzerijas* that serve them fresh from gas ovens are part of the landscape.

Another staple of any Mediterranean diet is pasta, but locally they like things with a twist. *Timpana*, a macaroni dish based in a tomato and meat sauce, is the favourite, and can be bought over the counter from vendors in most towns and villages. Wash

SWEET TREATS

Aside from savoury nibbles, there is no ignoring the local sweet tooth. Confectioners and speciality cafés brim with people keen to get their fix of delightful cakes, pastries and delicately made treats. *Konnoli ta' l-irkotta* (pastry cases filled with sweet ricotta) are truly delicious, and make the perfect teatime snack. Scrumptious *imqaret* (deep-fried date cakes) can be bought from side-of-the-road carts and are certainly addictive, but more than one can be hazardous to any cholesterol level. For something lighter, try a *Qaghaq ta' l'ghasel* (honey ring), a cir-

Right: frozen juices for sale in Valetta.

Left: Maltese bread is especially moreish.

opened back in 1933.
SEE ALSO BARS AND CAFÉS, P.34

C. Camilleri & Sons Ltd
49–51 Merchants Street, Valletta; tel: 2124 1642; www. camillerigroup.com; map p.132 B1
The place for sweets, this confectionery store was established in 1843 and to this day the family running it are still known as *Camilleri tal-Helu* (the sweet people). A great selection of individually wrapped sweets, chocolates and jellies.

Caffe Cordina
244/5 Republic Street, Valletta; tel: 2123 4385; www.caffe cordina.com; map p.132 B2
Right in the heart of Valletta, it was traditional for locals to flock here for afternoon tea. Recently renovated, they have maintained their reputation as an outlet for pastries, pies and cakes, and are best known for their tasty honey rings.
SEE ALSO BARS AND CAFÉS, P.33

City Gate Imqaret Stand
City Gate, Valletta; map p.132 A1
Seconds' walk from the bus

Pasta-loving locals relish a plate of traditional *ravjul* (ravioli); recipes have been found dating back to the 1200s! Stuffed with goat's cheese and parsley, they are usually served with a fresh basil and tomato sauce or deep-fried. For perfect *ravjul* try Oleander in Xaghra, Gozo *(see p.112).*

cle-shaped pastry made with treacle or honey that was traditionally eaten at Christmas but is now available all year round.

LOCAL SUPPLIERS
Busy Bee Cafe
7, Antonio Bosio Street, Ta Xbiex; tel: 2133 1738; www. busybee.com.mt; map p.135 E1
Despite becoming a household name, this popular café chooses to only have one outlet. Admittedly you will pay more than at most other cafés, but locals come from miles around to take-away their sweet ricotta-filled pastry cases which have been on the menu since Busy Bee first

Left: local goat's cheese.
Right: café dining.

chocolates every day in all shapes and sizes. Book well ahead around Easter.

Good Earth Health Food Shop
29, Main Street, Balluta Square, St Julian's; tel: 2134 1853; www.goodearth.com.mt; map p.135 D2
Health-conscious foodies should make this their first stop. Friendly staff will find you the right products to match your lifestyle whether you're looking for a vitamin boost, allergy solution or weight-loss aid.

Marsaxlokk Fish Market
Marsaxlokk Bay; map p.137 E2
Dozens of stalls line the pretty seafront of Marsaxlokk, stocking everything you need for a great meal from the freshest catches to fruit and vegetables. Get ready to haggle for your supper.

Master Wine Group
Oratory Street, Naxxar; tel: 2141 2391; www.master

station is a local gem – the tiny date cake stand. Deep-fat-fried these little cakes are irresistible and make the perfect snack, but do beware that your waistline may be in jeopardy!

Crystal Palace
St Paul's Street, Rabat; tel: 2145 3323; map p.134 C1
A blink-and-you'll-miss-it sort of place just outside Mdina. People flock to Crystal Palace for cheese and pea-filled *pastizzi*. Ignore the decor and instead soak up the local charm while sipping freshly

brewed tea from a glass (never a teacup). You'll find a friendly face behind the bar at most hours of the day and night, as the team rarely shut shop in order to keep up with the demand.

Fred's Sweets & Belgian Chocolates
University Street, Victoria, Gozo; tel: 2156 5131; map p.138 B3
Gozo may be the last place you'd expect to find a Belgian chocolatier, but find one you will. Fred, a Belgian now residing in Gozo, freshly prepares delicious

group.com.mt; map p.135 D2
One of the best selections
of wines, spirits and
liqueurs on the island. For
a local taste try a Malta-
made wine or the *Bajtra*
liqueur made from sweet
prickly pears.

Rubino
53, Old Bakery Street, Valletta;
tel: 2122 4656; map p.132 C3
A tiny restaurant that holds
delicious treasures. This is
Maltese food at its best,
and this eatery is particularly well known for its
desserts, including the traditional Casatella Siciliana,
a colourful cake made with
ricotta and covered in
marzipan.

Santa Lucia Cafe
Old Railway Track, Attard; tel:
2141 7894; www.santalucia
cafe.com; map p.135 D1
A great place if you want a

hamper of Maltese goodies.
A huge array of delicacies
sit behind glass counters.
Favourites include honey
rings and almond biscuits.

Stuzzico Deli
Merchant's Street, Valletta; tel:
2122 0025; map p.132 B1
Most large supermarkets
have a deli counter, but
nothing beats the real deal.
This is the perfect place
for cured meats, salamis,

cheeses and jarred goods.

Ta' Rikardu
4, Triq il-Fosos, Citadella,
Victoria; tel: 2155 5953;
map p.138 B3
Within the walled Citadella
in Victoria, Rikardu's is
something of an institution.
If you don't have time for
lunch, grab some jars of
local honey, goats' milk
cheeselets preserved in
vinegar and capers.

Left and right: fresh produce
for sale at local markets.

71

History

5200 BC
Arrival of man to Malta. It is likely that these settlers were originally from Sicily and presumably lived in caves. The islands still have pottery items dating back to this era.

3200 BC
Known as the temple period, numerous temples were built at this stage, many of which still stand today – now as some of the oldest structures in the world.

2000 BC
The invasion of Bronze Age peoples.

1000 BC
Malta is invaded by the Phoenicians, a population of sailors and merchants who came from the area today known as Lebanon.

720 BC
The Greeks founded a colony on Malta, called Melite (their word for honey).

480 BC
Carthaginian domination.

218 BC
The Romans occupied Malta and the islands flourished until the Vandals occupied the country in 440AD.

AD 60
St Paul is shipwrecked in the north of Malta, converting the Maltese people to Christianity.

533
Roman General Belisarius re-conquered Malta and Malta became part of the Roman province of Sicily.

870
Arabs occupy the islands. Traces of their impact are still notable in the local language and archaeology.

1090
Count Roger the Norman conquered Malta in 1090 and brought it back into the European fold.

1194 – 1350
In quick succession, Malta saw the domination of Swabia, France, Aragon, Catalonia and Castile.

1350
The Maltese nobility was established. During this time the population of Malta stood at around 9,000.

Below: Hagar Qim is just one of Malta's famous ancient temples.

1530

The Knights of the Order of St. John of Jerusalem arrived in Malta having been ousted from Rhodes by the Turks. Charles V suggested the move as an alternative. The knights were not impressed but came anyway and in March 1530, the Order was given Malta and Tripoli for the annual rent of a falcon (hence the legend of the Maltese Falcon.) The islands thrived.

1565

The Turks tried to capture the islands, but abandoned the attempt after they lost over 320 ships and had 30,000 of their soldiers killed, wounded or captured.

1566

Grand Master Jean de la Valette wants to build a fortified city; this eventually becomes the capital, Valletta.

1798

The Knights surrender Malta to Napoleon Bonaparte who ruled it until the Maltese revolted in 1800.

1814

Malta becomes a British Crown Colony and part of the British Empire.

1940–43

Malta also played a key role during World War II and defended itself very well. In fact the islands were granted the George Cross by King George for the bravery shown during numerous attacks and hardships.

1964

Malta becomes an independent country but remains part of the Commonwealth.

1974

Following an act of parliament, Malta becomes a Republic.

1979

The last British servicemen and women leave Malta.

2004

Following a local referendum, just over 53 percent of voters say yes to EU membership and Malta, along with nine other states, join the European Union.

2008

Malta joins the Eurozone.

2009

Architect Renzo Piano is chosen to inject new life into Valletta, including the rebuilding of the Opera House site which was bombed during World War II. It is a huge project, estimated for completion in 2015.

Hotels

Hotels in Malta average at around €120 per room per night, with varying facilities to suit all budgets. St Julian's and Sliema have long been the destinations of choice for those wanting to be in the thick of things, and both are great if you don't plan to hire a car. The islands are now home to many recognisable international chains and top hotels, many of them with in-house spas and massive pool decks, but unique and boutique accommodation options are also available if that's more your taste. Budget travellers will be pleased to know that the renowned Maltese hospitality doesn't limit itself to big spenders.

VALLETTA AND FLORIANA

British Hotel

40, Battery Street, Valletta; tel: 2122 4730; www.britishhotel. com; bus: 8; €; map p.135 E1

A throwback to those colonial days of yore. One of Malta's oldest family hotels, it is situated in quaint terraced streets and the service is friendly and welcoming. It's the ideal base to explore Malta, with rooftop sun deck and the restaurant's excellent flavours and cuisine presentation.

Excelsior Grand Hotel

Great Siege Road, Floriana; tel: 2125 0520; www.excelsior. com.mt; bus: 8; €€€; map p.135 E1

One of only two top hotels in the capital, this one certainly breaks the mould.

Prices are per room per night, with breakfast included (unless otherwise stated):
€ under €75
€€ €75–150
€€€ over €150

Above: Excelsior Grand Hotel.

The decor may be gaudy, but the service is spot on. Situated next to magnificent 16th-century bastions, you are only two minutes on foot to Valletta's gates and all the treasures it holds. With lots of natural light, fine dining, luxurious bath robes and 'sinkable' beds, Excelsior makes for a truly de luxe stay.

Grand Harbour Hotel

St Ursula Street, Valletta; tel: 2124 6003; www.grand harbourhotel.com; bus: 8; €; map p.132 C1

Seven floors of family-owned rooms with panoramic views of the Grand Harbour that defy the low price of staying here, even though accommodation and facilities are basic. The restaurant on the seventh floor offers decent, simple food and stunning sea views; the rooftop terrace is a great place to relax with a cool drink or snack.

Hotel Castille

Castille Square, Valletta; tel: 2124 3677; www.hotel castillemalta.com; bus: 8; €€; map p.132 A1

Originally built in the 16th century for the influential De Robertis family, Hotel Castille holds the elegance and beauty of a time gone by. Former stables are now a coffee shop, and the charming restaurant has a range of local and foreign cuisine. A great base, this hotel is just a quick walk from the Valletta bus terminus, the island's main shopping streets, a cinema, three

Left: Grand Harbour Hotel.

Jacuzzi. A good lower-budget option for those keen to stay within Valletta's walls.

SLIEMA, ST JULIAN'S & PACEVILLE

Corinthia Marina

St George's Bay, St Julian's; tel: 2138 1719; www.corinthia hotels.com; bus: 62, 64, 66, 68; €€; map p.135 E2

Started 40 years ago as a family business in a villa, hospitality here comes as second nature. The large windows make the rooms airy, and all have a spacious terrace to relax and enjoy the view. One of the island's top four-star hotels, it enjoys an excellent location just minutes walk from the newly regenerated St George's Bay beach *(see p.38)*, and excellent facilities.

Corinthia San Gorg

St George's Bay, St Julian's; tel: 2137 4114; www.corinthia hotels.com; bus: 62, 64, 66, 68; €€; map p.135 D2

The now world-renowned Corinthia chain started in Malta and went on to build its name in several other parts of the globe. This is one of their flagships and, although it's getting on a bit, is still a delightful place to stay and truly relax. The great thing about this hotel is that, despite its close proximity to the entertainment mecca Paceville, guests can still feel secluded and away from it all. A superb lower-budget option that still retains all the glitz and facilities of a five-star.

Somewhat surprisingly, the capital Valletta lacks many top hotels and resorts, and visitors are often reluctant to stay here. That said, the city is perfect for those keen to immerse themselves in history or those wanting to step back from the bustle of traditional tourist resorts. Although there are no beaches nearby, Valletta boasts top restaurants and activities to keep the whole family happy.

theatres and umpteen top eateries.

Hotel Phoenicia

The Mall, Floriana; tel: 2122 5241; www.phoenicia malta.com; bus: 8; €€€; map p.135 E1

One of the most established hotels on the islands. By choosing the Phoenicia you're opting to get truly immersed in the history of the place. Recently renovated, but still staying true to the subdued colours of its charming Art Deco style, this Mediterranean base offers all the luxuries you'll

need for a unique stay, including classic paintings, stunning sea and city views and large French windows.

Osborne Hotel

South Street, Valletta; tel: 2124 3656; www.osbornehotel.com; bus: 8; €; map p.132 A2

Inside a magnificent palace built by St John, you are a stone's throw away from all of the city's major attractions. The rooftop terrace is stunning with its view of Marsamxett harbour, swim-spa and large

Left: Corinthia San Gorg.

Left: Hilton Malta. **Right:** Le Méridien St Julian's.

Prices are per room per night, with breakfast included (unless otherwise stated):
€ under €75
€€ €75–150
€€€ over €150

The Diplomat Hotel

173, Tower Road, Sliema; tel: 2349 7000; www.diplomat. com.mt; bus: 62, 64, 66, 68; €; map p.135 E2

Just minutes' walk from the Sliema café strip, the Ferries and the bus terminus, try to secure a seaview room. A great budget option for a bed in the city, but bear in mind breakfast is extra.

Fortina Spa Resort

Tigne Seafront; Sliema; tel: 2346 0000; www.hotel

fortina.com; bus: 62, 64, 66, 68; €€€; map p.135 E2

Malta's newest high-rise hotel, with five swimming pools, a fitness centre and some of the best spa treatments on the islands. Their Therapeutic Spa Bedrooms (the first in the world) boast in-room Jacuzzis, steam showers and Dermalife machines. The fact that this is an all-inclusive, down to the tasty cocktails at happy hour, simply adds to the fun.

Golden Tulip Vivaldi

Dragonara Road, St Julian's; tel: 2137 8100; www.golden tulipvivaldi.com; bus: 62, 64, 66, 68; €€€; map p.135 D2

If 'in the thick of things' sums up your desires for a holiday location, then this one's for you. This four-star hotel is smack-bang in the middle of Malta's main entertainment spot, but still retains some sense luxury and calm. The interior is reminiscent of a Venetian palace, and simply adds to the uniqueness of this city location.

Hilton Malta

Portomaso, St Julian's; tel: 2138 3383; www.malta. hilton.com; bus: 62, 64, 66, 68; €€€; map p.135 D2

Probably the most sought-after postcode in Malta, Portomaso is a hub of luxury for those who enjoy the finer things. As is to be expected from a Hilton, this hotel boasts all the best facilities, and the rooms are chic and comfortable; treat yourself to a de luxe plus room for spectacular sea views. Dining is one of the highlights of staying here, with both Mediterranean and oriental flavours on offer.

Hotel Juliani

12, St George's Road, St Julian's; tel: 2138 8000;

THE VIVALDI

Left: Golden Tulip Vivaldi.

www.hoteljuliani.com; bus: 62, 64, 66, 68; map p.135 D2

A beautifully decorated boutique hotel that brings the charm of the Mediterranean in. The clean lines inside blend with touches of past times to make this converted sea-front town house a unique stay. You can enjoy a view of Malta's traditional colourful fishing boats bobbing in the harbour, and the food is great too.

Intercontinental Hotel
St George's Bay, St Julian's; tel: 2137 7600; www.ichotels group.com; bus: 62, 64, 66, 68; €€€; map p.135 E2

Seconds' walk from the Baystreet shopping complex and all of the island's top pubs and club, this hotel is also within relatively easy reach of the island's historic and cultural sites. Modern and fresh, this waterfront resort has a private beach and water-sports facilities, and is just five minutes' walk from the picturesque Spinola Bay and all its restaurants.

Kennedy Nova
116, The Strand, Sliema; tel: 2134 5480; www.kennedy nova.com; bus: 62, 64, 66, 68; €€; map p.135 E2

This family-run establishment has been popular since the 1960s. With views over to the Valletta Bastions, it makes a great base. With friendly staff and comfortable accommodation, the price is quite right too.

Le Méridien St Julian's
39, Main Street, Balluta Bay, St Julian's; tel: 2311 0000; www.starwoodhotels.com/ lemeridien; bus: 62, 64, 66, 68; €€€; map p.135 E2

Within easy reach of both St Julian's and Sliema, this new, expansive and expertly decorated resort is set on pretty Balluta Bay. The rooms are larger than average and the facilities excellent; you can even bring your dog! There are exceptional in-house dining options and a lovely reception lounge with free Wifi for guests.

The Palace
High Street, Sliema; tel: 2133 3444; www.thepalacemalta. com; bus: 62, 64, 66, 68; €€; map p.135 E2

One of the newer hotels, The Palace is distinctive and stylish. Enjoy the sunbathing area, swimming pool and lounge bar, as well as the unbeatable views from the rooftop restaurant. Rooms are fun and spacious, with special accommodation including the Music Room for those wanting to jive or bop through their holiday. Breakfast is not included.

Preluna Hotel & Spa
Tower Road, Sliema; tel: 2133 4001; www.preluna-hotel.com; bus: 62, 64, 66, 68; €€; map p.135 E2

Turn one way for picturesque Spinola Bay and the other for the island's buzzing commercial centre. Recently renovated, this is one way to enjoy good accommodation in the heart of Sliema, without breaking the bank. Enjoy the La Piazza bar and barman Anthony's

77

Above: Victoria Hotel.

repartee, or the top-floor sushi bar Cafe Sakura.

Radisson SAS Bay Point Resort

St George's Bay, St Julian's; tel: 2137 4894; www.radisson. com.mt; bus: 62, 64, 66, 68; €€; map p.135 E2
Situated in a secluded bay yet also within easy walking distance of Paceville's vibrant nightlife options, this is one of those hotels that has it all. Highlights include the large pool area, private beach and the restaurants – one of which is open 24 hours a day,

just in case you get a tad peckish at an odd hour.

Rafael Spinola Hotel

Upper Ross Street, St Julian's; tel: 2137 4488; www.rafael spinolamalta.com; bus: 62, 64, 66, 68; €€; map p.135 D2
This hotel is within walking distance of the island's most sought-after waterfront destinations and two minutes from a bus stop that ensures you can explore the rest of the country easily. Basic, but comfortable and modern with some sea-view rooms.

The Victoria Hotel

Gorg Gorg Olivier Street, Sliema; tel: 2133 4711; www.victoriahotel.com; bus: 62, 64, 66, 68; €; map p.135 E2
Highlights here include huge balconies ideal for lounging on and friendly staff who will go out of their way to facilitate your stay. Rooms are either fresh Mediterranean blue or rich Victorian mahogany, and for a bit

Right: the fantastic Westin Dragonara pool.

extra, indulge in a luxury suite. Breakfast is not included.

Westin Dragonara Resort

Dragonara Road, St Julian's; tel: 2138 1000; www.westin malta.com; bus: 62, 64, 66, 68; €€€; map p.135 D2
Located on a private peninsula, you're promised a relaxing stay overlooking unobstructed views of the Mediterranean. Especially suited to families, there is a good-sized family pool and a kids' club. Enjoy the superb food on offer, starting with the lavish buffet served on the terrace.

MDINA, RABAT, DINGLI
Point de Vue Guesthouse

2/7 Saqqajja Square, Rabat; tel: 2145 4117; www.pointdevue malta.com; bus: 81; €; map p.134 C1
This historic guesthouse does what it says on the tin, offering accommoda-

tion with great views. A convenient location from where to explore the rest of the Malta. Breakfast will really hit the spot too.

Xara Palace Relais & Châteaux
Council Square, Mdina; tel: 2145 0560; www.xara palace.com.mt; bus: 80, 81, 84; €€€; map p.134 C1
A boutique hotel in a grand old building, in one of the island's most historic spots – the Xara Palace team are known for their unabashed hospitality. Highlights include the beautiful inner courtyard and double-level rooms featuring a spiral staircase. Full of charm as well as luxury, it will make you feel like you're stepping back in time.

THE CENTRE
Corinthia Palace Hotel & Spa
De Paule Avenue, Balzan; tel: 2144 0301; www.corinthia. com; bus: 80, 81; €€; map

Left: Radisson SAS Golden Sands, *(see p.80).*

p.135 D1
Set in the landscaped gardens of a 19th-century restored villa; basing yourself in Attard means you're close to Valletta and much of the rest of the island. Boasting one of the island's best spas, this is a great get-away-from-it-all hotel, with a lovely outdoor pool and great food.

BAHAR IC-CAGHAQ, BUGIBBA AND ST PAUL'S BAY
Dolmen Resort Hotel
Dolmen Street, Bugibba; tel: 2355 2355; www.dolmen.

> Renting a farmhouse is the local answer to self-catering, and there are many to choose from both in Malta and Gozo. Great for families who want to do their own thing, most will have private swimming facilities, as well as spacious living areas and air-conditioning. Be sure to enquire about the facilities beforehand and to ask to see pictures or a video of the residence. Check out: www.farmhousemalta.com or www.gozofarmhouses.com.

> Prices are per room per night, with breakfast included (unless otherwise stated):
> € under €75
> €€ €75–150
> €€€ over €150

com.mt; bus: 49; €€; map p.134 C3
The facilities of this massive waterfront resort include four swimming pools, one especially for children, and a newly designed spa with state-of-the-art therapy rooms. We like the daily buffet, and this hotel's close proximity to the sea.

Suncrest Hotel
Qawra Coast Road, Qawra; tel: 2157 7101; www.suncrest hotel.com; bus: 48, 49, 58, 652; €; map p.135 C3
The famous waterfall may be gone, but the ornate reception is still here. Sea views are extra, but the fact that this hotel is now all-inclusive makes it quite good value. A healthy breakfast is served until 11.30am – perfect for those relaxing lie-ins.

79

Prices are per room per night, with breakfast included (unless otherwise stated):
€ under €75
€€ €75–150
€€€ over €150

If it's sandy beaches you want, stay in the north. The resorts in this region are tailored to families with children keen to get their buckets and spades out, and most will offer a free shuttle bus to the shore if they're not within easy walking distance.

THE NORTH

Hotel Riu Seabank

Marfa Road, Mellieha; tel: 2152 1460; www.seabankhotel.com; bus: 44, 45; €€; map p.134 B3

A good base in the north, with all the facilities you'd expect from a four-star resort. Great for families, with plenty of activities to keep children busy, and Mellieha Bay, the island's most popular sandy beach, is only a stone's throw away.

Radisson SAS Golden Sands Resort & Spa

Golden Bay, Mellieha; tel: 2356 1000; www.goldensands. malta.radissonsas.com; bus: 47; €€€; map p.134 B3

One of the best hotels on the island. With stunning views out over one of the

Above: Radisson Golden Sands.

most beautiful parts of Malta, great facilities and a private sandy beach, you'd be hard pushed to do better for an idyllic getaway.

Riviera Resort & Spa

Marfa Bay, Mellieha; tel: 2152 5900; www.riviera.com.mt; bus: 45; €€; map p.134 B3

Set on Malta's northern-most point, with views of Comino and Gozo, this is a great base if you also hope to explore the sister islands. Good food, comfortable rooms, a really

good-sized pool and a sandy beach perfect for paddling all seal the deal.

GOZO AND COMINO

Comino Hotel

San Niklaw Bay, Comino; tel: 2152 9821; www.comino hotel.com; €€; map p.139 E1

You take a boat to get here and find yourself on a pretty, deserted island with only a few other hotel guests for company. If you want to switch off, do it here. The accommodation is basic, but the away-from-it-all aura is unbeatable.

Hotel Calypso

Marsalforn Bay, Marsalforn; tel:

2156 2000; www.hotelcalypso
gozo.com; bus: 21; €€; map
p.138 C4
Recently refurbished, Hotel
Calypso is one of the oldest hotels on the island. A
great place for a holiday,
the rooms are fresh with
everything you need to
relax, and the views are
stunning. The sea-view
rooms, with their own private balconies, are worth
the added extra.

Hotel ta Cenc
Sannat, Gozo; tel: 2155 6819;
www.vjborg.com; bus: 91;
€€€; map p.138 B2
Something completely out
of the ordinary, this eco-
chic hotel is set in acres
of untouched grounds

Left: Hotel Riu Seabank.
Above: Kempinski San
Lawrenz Resort.

and has incredible views
out over the Mediter-
ranean. Accommodation
is original – bungalows
with their own private ter-
races, and the facilities
are good. Admittedly
most of the rooms are
due an upgrade, but opt
for the new luxury suites if
you're in the mood for
perfection.

Kempinski San Lawrenz Resort
Rokon Street, San Lawrenz,
Gozo; tel: 2211 0000;
www.kempinski-gozo.com;
bus: 91; €€; map p.138 A3
Another eco-focused
resort, the Kempinski is a
haven for those after a
hotel with a great spa and
lush grounds to explore.
The food is to die for, and
the rooms well kept and
comfortable.

Maria Giovanna Hostel
41, Rabat Road, Marsalforn; tel:
www.tamariagozo.com; bus:
21; €; map p.138 C4
A welcoming home away
from home, this family-run
guesthouse was recently
upgraded from a hostel.
Enjoy the hospitable
atmosphere and your 200-
year-old surroundings,
which make the perfect
base on a budget.

Gozo has become a holiday
destination in its own right, and
its hotels reflect that. As
Malta's smaller, greener sister,
there is an eco-feel to the place
and hotels are generally more
eco-chic here as well. **Hotel Ta
Cenc** and the **Kempinski San
Lawrenz Resort**, in particular,
are super places to stay if
you're conscious of your
carbon footprint.

81

Language

English, one of the islands' two official languages, is spoken by most people in Malta. The older generation learn it while the British were stationed here and younger people are exposed to it from their first day at school. Recognised officially since 1934, Maltese descended from Siculo-Arabic (the Arabic dialect that developed across parts of the Mediterranean) and is the only Semitic language which is written in the Roman alphabet. Italian is also widely spoken, partly due to Italy's close proximity to the islands and partly because Italian television was the only sort available until about 15 years ago.

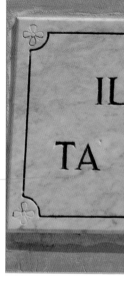

first known Maltese dictionary was written by the French Knight François de Vion Thézan Court in 1640. In the 19th century Mikiel Anton Vassalli, a linguist, made a concerted effort to transcribe spoken Maltese in a comprehensive written form, and he has since been recognised as the father of the Maltese language.

Under British rule Maltese came under threat and children were even punished for speaking it at school. Today the islanders are fiercely protective of it and strive to retain it; as a result it is now listed as an official language of the EU.

THE MALTESE ALPHABET

The Maltese alphabet is based on the Latin alphabet with the addition of some letters, making it a 30-letter alphabet.

The letter 'y' does not exist in the Maltese alphabet and is replaced by 'j'.

THE HISTORY OF THE LANGUAGE

Over the centuries the Phoenicians, Carthaginians and Romans all contributed bits and bobs to the development of Maltese, which is why it is a language all of its own. But it was actually the invasion of the Arabs that had the most profound effect (an effect which can still be heard today), and thus it morphed into a Semitic language, written in the Latin alphabet with a dash of Italian and French and a few English words thrown in for good measure. The result reflects layers of different influences to an extraordinary extent.

The oldest known document in Maltese is *Il Cantilena*, a poem from the 15th century, and the

ASTJUN
N MIKIEL

Left: Maltese is the only Semitic language written in the Roman alphabet.

Bad *Hazin*
Thank you (very much)!
Grazzi (hafna)!
Nice to meet you!
Ghandi pjacir!
What's your name?
X'jismek?
My name is...
Jien jisimni...
I'm lost *Intlift*
Do you speak English?
Titkellem bl-Ingliz?
Can you help me?
Tista tghini?
How much is this?
Kemm jiswa dan?
I don't understand!
Mhux nifhem!
Big/Small *Kbir/zghir*
Today/Now *Illum/Issa*
Tomorrow/Yesterday
Ghada/Ilbierah
Yes/No *Iva/le*

Locals are forever using **Maltenglish**, or Minglish, as opposed to the complete form of either language. Both words refer to the way locals code-switch between the two and have thus created another language all of their own. Local English-speakers love the raw quality of some Maltese words and will throw them into their speech. Meanwhile, Maltese lacks certain technical terms and expressions, so Maltese-speakers will happily add English terms to the mix. It's estimated that at least a third of the population uses Minglish regularly, so don't be surprised if you can't resist doing the same!

I'm fine, thanks!
Tajjeb, grazzi!
And you? *U int?*
Good/So-so *Tajjeb/Imsomma*

USEFUL PHRASES
Good morning!
L-ghodwa t-tajba/Bongu
Good evening!
Wara nofs inhar it-tajjeb
Welcome! (to greet someone) *Merhba*
How are you? *Kif int?*

Left and right: traditional living keeps the Maltese language alive.

83

Museums

With such an eclectic and vibrant past, the Maltese Islands have plenty of interesting and entertaining museums to choose from. The majority of the history-related exhibits are based around the Valletta, Mdina and Three Cities areas; all three were strongholds of the Knights of St John, and several museums are housed in buildings constructed by the Knights themselves, simply adding to the long list of reasons to visit them. Vital aspects of the islands' destiny were dictated by the events of World War II, and numerous museums also chart the goings-on of those dark days.

VALLETTA AND FLORIANA

Casa Rocca Piccola
74, Republic Street, Valletta; tel: 2122 1499; www.casarocca piccola.com; Mon–Sat 10am–4pm; under-12s free; map p.133 C3

This privately owned family home was given to the 9th Marquis and Marchioness de Piro. Today the intricately decorated house offers a unique historical insight into the customs and traditions of Malta over the last 400 years. With over 50 rooms and collections of silver and paintings, the house is spectacular and also per-

Valletta, a World Heritage Site, has often been described as an 'open-air museum'. There are countless attractions to visit in the city, but as you wander between them, take the time to admire Valletta itself and to discover the true hidden gems of architectural and historic value left behind by the numerous peoples who have cultivated it.

fect for sparking the imaginations of little ones.

Grand Master's Palace Armoury
Grand Master's Palace, Merchants' Street, Valletta; tel: 2124 9349; www.heritage malta.com; daily 9am–5pm; charge; map p.132 C2

This collection of the world's greatest arms is one of Europe's most important historic monuments with regard to cul-

Left: exhibit from the National Museum of Archaeology.

ture. Authentic pieces from the period of the Great Siege in 1565 include arms trophies. Mysterious and interesting, the armoury is worth exploring and will be enjoyed by visitors of all ages.

Manoel Theatre Museum
115, Old Theatre Street, Valletta; tel: 2122 2618; www.teatrumanoel.com.mt; guided tours: Mon–Fri 10.15am–3.30pm, Sat 10.15am–12.30pm every 45 mins; charge; map p.132 B3

This majestic theatre displays a large amount of beautiful exhibits donated by generous private collectors. The museum is a tribute to three centuries of theatrical history on the Maltese Islands, and despite being of modest size, the display room richly depicts a vast history. A highlight is the section dedicated to the Opera House that was

Left: St John's Co-Cathedral.

paintings by leading local and internationally acclaimed artists, Maltese silverware, marble statuary, bronze and wood furniture items and majolica pieces.

National War Museum

Fort St Elmo, Valletta; tel: 2122 2430; www.heritagemalta.org; daily 9am–5pm; charge; map p.133 D4

Set in an old drill hall, the focus is on the two world wars, and this exhibition traces the events of the developments and major occurrences with their local and foreign consequences. The museum concentrates on the role of Malta, with a memorial at the end dedicated to those who lost their lives.

St John's Co-Cathedral & Museum

St John's Square, Valletta; tel: 2122 0536; www.stjohnsco cathedral.com; Mon–Fri 9.30am–4.30pm, Sat 9.30am–12.30pm; under-12s free; map p.132 B2

In this Baroque-style structure you'll find donated gifts of high artistic value from Grand Mas-

---

Here for a fleeting visit with no real time to explore? **The Malta Experience** (St Elmo Bastions, Valletta; tel: 2124 3776; shows are hourly from 11am–4pm Mon–Fri and 11am–2pm Sat–Sun; adult €9.50, students €6.50, under 14s €4.50; map p.133 E4) audiovisual experience in Valletta offers an enjoyable dip into history, covering 7,000 years in 50 minutes of big-screen action.

destroyed in World War II.
SEE ALSO CULTURAL ACTIVITES, P.52

National Museum of Archaeology

Auberge de Provence, Republic Street, Valletta; tel: 2122 1623; www.heritagemalta.org; daily 9am–7pm; charge; map p.132 B2

Dating back to Malta's Neolithic period, the exhibited artefacts in this museum span from the Ghar Dalam phase (5200 BC) to the Tarxien phase

(2500 BC). Here you can see the earliest tools used by prehistoric people, and a highlight is the 'Sleeping Lady' from the Hagar Qim *(see also p.121)*.

National Museum of Fine Arts

South Street, Valletta; tel: 2122 5769; www.heritagemalta.org; daily 9am–5pm; charge; map p.132 A2

This multifaceted display of Maltese art shows works dating from late medieval times to the present day and features

Right: the Grand Master's Palace Armoury.

Square, Mdina; tel: 2145 5951; www.heritagemalta.org; daily 9am–5pm; charge; map p.134 C1

Life and earth sciences are represented in this national repository of biological examples, focusing mainly on the Maltese Islands. This exhibition covers human evolution, insects, birds and marine ecosystems, a highlight being the display of over 1 million species of shell.

Palazzo Falson Historic House Museum
Villegaignon Street, Mdina; tel: 2145 4512; www.palazzo falson.com; Tue–Sun 10am–5pm; charge; bus: 80, 81, 84; map p.134 C1
The former home of Captain Olof Frederick Gollocher, this two-storey medieval palace is now a shrine to his extensive

ters and several Knights, Caravaggio's *The Beheading of St John the Baptist* being one – the largest known painting by the artist. The carved elaborate architectural design gives the cathedral its character.
SEE ALSO CHURCHES, P.44

Toy Museum
222, Republic Street, Valletta; tel: 2125 1652; Mon–Fri 10am–3pm; children free; map p.132 B2
Comprising three floors, this museum showcases an extensive and impressive myriad of toys dating back from the 1950s onwards. Of particular interest may be the collection of Corgy, Dinky and Matchbox cars. Great for a wander down memory lane, and children will love it.

MDINA, RABAT AND DINGLI
Mdina Cathedral Museum
Archbishop Square, Mdina; tel: 2145 4697; Mon–Fri 9.30am–4.30pm, Sat 9.30am–3.30pm; under-12s free; map p.134 C1
The original cathedral dated back to the 13th century but was destroyed during the earthquake of 1693. The new Baroque church that is seen today has risen in its place. The museum features treasures salvaged from the destruction: a collection of paintings, prints, woodcuts and Old Master drawings, all the legacy of Count Saverio Marchese (1757–1833).
SEE ALSO CHURCHES, P.46

National Museum of Natural History
Vilhena Palace, St Publius

collection of arts and antiques. The collection shows years of passion for *objets d'art*, and is a rich display for the public to peruse. Look out for the beautiful collection of personal photos that truly shed light on this eccentric but loveable fellow.

SEE ALSO ARCHITECTURE, P.29

The Roman Villa

Museum Esplanade, Rabat; tel: 2145 4125; www.heritage malta.org; daily 9am–5pm; charge; map p.134 C1

The villa depicts the life of the Romans with glimpses into their cooking, weaving, body care and entertainment. The site features a Muslim cemetery built over the remains of a Roman townhouse, plus a display of uncovered artefacts, an olive-pipper, found in Marsaxlokk, and fragments of flourmills and tombstones.

THE CENTRE
Malta Aviation Museum

Ta' Qali; tel: 2141 6095; www. maltaaviationmuseum.com; daily 9am–5pm; charge; bus: 65, 80, 81, 86; map p.134 C1

The aircraft displays give a unique insight into Malta's rich aviation history. By acquiring, restoring and preserving aircrafts, artefacts and cultural and historical documentation, the museum boasts an interesting and eye-opening exhibition. Exhibits include the Fairey Swordfish, Tiger Moth, Submarine Spitfire and Hawker Hurricane. There is even an English Electric Lightning donated by one very impressed visitor, and engines used in World War II.

Palazzo Parisio

Victory Square, Naxxar; tel: 2141 2461; www.palazzo parisio.com; daily 9am–6pm, guided tours on the hour until 1pm; charge; map p.135 D2

Set in beautiful, landscaped gardens, this palace was acquired in the 19th century by Marquis Giuseppe Scicluna and still remains in the family, now owned by the Baroness of

Left: outside the National Museum of Natural History.

87

Left: Palazzo Parisio.

Originally erected in the 1530s, the Inquisitor's Palace has seen much change over the centuries. It became the official residence of the first inquisitor, Magistrate Pietro Dusina, in 1574, and underwent much transformation until the mid-18th century, when it was turned into a typically Roman palace. Restored again in 1966, it is now home to the Museum of Ethnography, and the display areas include the tribunal room, the prison complex and the kitchen.
SEE ALSO ARCHITECTURE, P.27

The Malta at War Museum

Couvre Porte Gate, Vittoriosa; tel: 2189 6617; www.wirtartna.org; 9.30am–5pm, guided tours every hour; charge; map p.135 E1
The museum focuses on the hardships faced by the Maltese nation throughout World War II and concentrates largely on the Maltese civilians affected by the conflict. There are guided tours of the rehabilitated rooms and underground air-raid shelter which offer stark insight into what life must have been like.

Malta Maritime Museum

Ex-Naval Bakery, Vittoriosa; tel: 2166 0052; www.heritagemalta.org; daily 9am–5pm; charge; map p.135 E1
Housed in an old naval bakery, Malta's maritime museum charts the island's history, presenting the global nature of seafaring and its impact on society. There are numerous artefacts on display high-

Tabria. Described as 'a miniature Versailles', visitors can absorb the exuberance of the marble, mirrored walls, rare paintings and extravagant gilding. The garden, one of the lushest in Malta, is a sight to behold in itself, and many happy hours can be spent wandering around it before stopping for tea in the delightful **Café Luna**.
SEE ALSO CAFÉS, P.35; PARKS AND GARDENS, P.103

BAHAR IC-CAGHAQ, BUGIBBA AND ST PAUL'S
Malta Classic Car Museum

Tourist Street, Bugibba; tel: 2157 8885; www.classiccarsmalta.com; Mon–Fri 9.30am–6pm, Sat–Sun 9.30am–1.30pm; charge; map p.135 C3
This tribute to the automobile industry, spread over approximately 3,000 sq m (33,000 sq ft), features a 'living' collection of automobiles that is regularly updated. You can see the classics – Alfa Romeo, Austin, Jaguar – and also motorbikes – Lambretta and Vespa. You can even pick up a collectable model car from the gift shop's eclectic assortment.

THE THREE CITIES
The Inquisitor's Palace

Main Gate Street, Vittoriosa; tel: 2182 7006; www.heritagemalta.org; daily 9am–5pm; charge; map p.135 E1

The majority of Malta's museums are located in its historic spots, and the same can be said of Gozo – so head straight to the **Citadella** to get your history fix. Within the walls of this tiny fortified town you'll find the Cathedral Museum, the Museum of Archaeology, the Folklore Museum, the Citadel Armoury, the Natural Science Museum and the Old Prison.

Above and below: Malta Classic Car Museum.

lighting the different epochs.

GOZO AND COMINO
Folklore Museum
Bernardo de Opuo Street, Citadella, Victoria, Gozo; tel: 2156 2034; 9am–5pm; charge; map p.138 B2

This museum presents a wide range of exhibits concerning the domestic, traditional and rural ways of life in Gozo and Malta. A whole room is dedicated to the fishing industry, while other displays include rural trades such as agriculture and stonemasonry, and Gozitan crafts, namely lace-making.

Gharb Folklore Museum
99, Church Square, Gharb, Gozo; tel: 2156 1929; Mon–Sat 9am–4pm, Sun 9am–1pm; charge; bus: 2, 91; map p.138 A3

Exhibited in this 28-roomed 18th-century, historical house is the history of Gozitan times gone by. The privately owned house features a miller's room, antique press room, carpenter's workshop and an array of Gozo's memories. Despite some diverse items, the museum focuses more on the prominent crafts and trades of the Maltese Islands.

Gozo Cathedral Museum
Cathedral Square, Citadella, Victoria, Gozo; tel: 2155 6087; www.gozocathedral.org.mt; Mon–Sat 10.30–4.30pm; map p.138 B2

The awe-inspiring facade of this beautiful cathedral dominates the small, irregularly shaped square that it sits in. Built entirely from local limestone in a Mediterranean Baroque style, the cathedral oozes cultural charm. Quoin plasters and inverted urn finials

Left and below: Gozo's Museum of Archaeology.

charge; map p.138 B2
The museum is situated within the walls of the Citadella just behind the old gate. There is a chronological depiction of the cultural history of Gozo inside this 17th-century townhouse, from prehistory to the early modern period. It features stick figurines found at the burial place of the Xaghra stone circle between 3150 BC and 2500 BC.

frame the ornate design. Note the marble coats of arms of Grand Master Ramon Perellos (1697–1720) and Bishop David Cocco-Palmeri (1684–1711) with the present Bishop of Gozo in the centre.
SEE ALSO CHURCHES, P.49

Maritime Museum
Parish Priest Street, Nadur, Gozo; tel: 2156 5226; Mon–Sat 9am–4.45pm; charge; map p.139 D2
One-time primary school teacher Kelinu Galea collected maritime memora-

bilia for 65 years and built up this impressive exhibition. It contains extremely rare exhibits such as authentic timber from Lord Nelson's ship HMS *Victory*, and the first US warship. Amongst the models, uniforms, photos and vessel parts are the gold epaulettes that Mountbatten wore during his period of duty.

Museum of Archaeology
Citadella, Victoria, Gozo; tel: 2155 6144; www.heritage malta.org; daily 9am–5pm;

Museum of Toys
10, Gnien Xibla Street, Xaghra, Gozo; tel: 2156 2489; Apr: Thur–Sat 10am–1pm, May–Oct: Mon–Sat 10am–noon, 3–6pm, winter/public holidays 10am–1pm; bus: 64, 65; charge; map p.138 C3
This collection began with one doll and now features toys from all around the world. Highlights include a late 18th-century Maltese doll with a carved wooden head, a 100-year-

old pressed paper 'Hunting Scene' and clockwork tin toys from the 1920s and 30s.

Natural Science Museum

Citadella, Victoria, Gozo; tel: 2155 6153; www.heritage malta.org; daily 9am–5pm; charge; map p.138 B2

Located inside the Citadella, in a cluster of 17th-century houses, this museum features collections linked to the island's geology, minerals, marine life, insects, local habitats and ecosystems. A highlight is a moonstone fragment brought back by the Apollo II 1969 crew.

The Old Prison

Cathedral Square, Citadella, Victoria, Gozo; tel: 2156 5988; www.heritagemalta.org; daily 9am–5pm; charge; map p.138 B2

In use between the 16th and 20th centuries, the prison is split into two sections: an entrance hall previously used as a common cell and a free-standing block with six individual cells. Note the graffiti on the walls of the cells with representations of ships, stars, hand profiles and names.

Ta' Kola Windmill

Bambina Street, Xaghra, Gozo; tel: 2156 1071; daily 5–7pm; charge; map p.138 C3

Meaning 'Nicholas's Windmill', Ta' Kola Windmill dates back to the trade of the miller and gives an overview of the rural economy and domestic past of Gozo. It features a 15m (49ft) tower built by St John, one of 12 to survive, and a display of tools with the miller's living quarters.

Right: Ta' Kola Windmill.
Above: Malta Aviation Museum, *see p.87.*

Nightlife

While the Maltese Islands probably don't scream 'pumping' at you instantly, you may be surprised by the amount of after-dark options available. Paceville, the island's own little Ibiza, is a mecca of pubs, clubs and nightspots that stays lively until the wee hours all year round. If you enjoy wall-to-wall people then this is the place for you, especially in the summer months when it is overrun with clubbers out to have a great time. Bugibba is another hotspot – best known for its British-style pubs and karaoke bars where every night is party night and 'cheesy' is the order of the day. *See also Bars and Cafés, p.30–35.*

VALLETTA AND FLORIANA

222

Great Siege Road, Valletta; tel: 2733 3222; www.two-twenty two.com; daily 7.30–11pm, Fri–Sun until 1am; map p.132 A3

This unique dining, music and cultural experience owes its ever-flowing atmosphere to the musicians, creative thinkers and artists who are welcomed in with open arms. In this constant hub of activity, dining and drinking is a whole new concept set in beautiful glass surroundings overlooking the Marsamxett Harbour. Popular with the local IT crowd, it is usually lively until late, especially at the weekend.

Hard Rock

Valletta Waterfront; tel: 2123 3346; www.hardrock.com; 10am–1am; map p.133 D1

The Hard Rock brand came to Malta several years ago, and the locals haven't looked back – they love its tongue-in-cheek

Above: Valletta as night falls.

blend of cocktails and rowdy music. Aside from the American menu for those after a bite, the outdoor terrace is usually alive with dancing or live music.

Q Bar

Vault 1, Valletta Waterfront; www.qbar.com.mt; May–Oct daily 6.30pm–4am, Nov–Apr Tue–Sun 6.30pm–4am; map p.133 D1

One of Malta's latest and most intriguing lounge-bar concepts, this venue challenges the ordinary bar experience and caters for a range of generations with its chic decor and range of

music styles. Recline on the waterfront terrace enjoying a premium glass of wine and delicious platter of assorted mezedes, sushi and salad, or for a livelier atmosphere, head into the trendy interior to absorb music from renowned DJs.

SLIEMA, ST JULIAN'S AND PACEVILLE

Axis

Triq San Gorg, Paceville; tel: 2135 8078; www.axis.com.mt; daily 9pm–1am, Fri–Sat until 4am; charge; map p.135 E2

The granddaddy of all local clubs, Axis has seen generations through their party days. This massive venue comprises three areas – Axis, Matrix and Styx, each with remarkable sound systems. Axis has hosted some of Europe's top DJs, including Judge Jules and members of the Ministry of Sound. With impressive laser shows and music ranging from commercial and R&B to house and elec-

Left: Malta's nightlife has a lot to offer.

and efficient service at the bar, this it is a unique venue with added spice.

Havana
82, St George's Road, Paceville; tel: 2137 4500; www.havana malta.com; daily; free; map p.135 E2

Said to be the largest hip hop, soul and R&B venue on the island, Havana has a 3,000-person capacity and comprises two floors of luxurious surroundings, including large sweeping bars and expansive dance floors. A visit to the bar won't set you back too far, and there is an array of cocktails to choose from. An open-air terrace spans the entire front of the second floor.

Huggins Restaurant and Wine Lodge
Dragonara Road, Paceville; tel: 2137 5443; daily 9am– midnight; map p.135 E2

With wooden interiors, this two-floor bar and wine lodge in the heart of Paceville regularly features local DJs and is a great place to hangout with friends. If the dance floor isn't calling to you, maybe the menu will, as the bar

If you want a crash course in Maltese clubbing, head to **Paceville**, the capital of the local nightlife scene. Once a mere cluster of bars frequented by the British stationed here, it is now the best place for late-night clubs, Irish bars and dancing... lots and lots of dancing.

tro, this club attracts large crowds, making for an energetic and busy atmosphere.

Blackgold
94, Ix Xatt, Sliema; tel: 2133 4808; daily 9am–1am; map p.135 E2

A good stop-off point before you hit the St Julian's clubs, Blackgold is a relaxed and popular haunt. Busy at the weekend, it can be hard to find a seat indoors, but you can always opt to head outside to mix with the eclectic crowd that con-

Right: upmarket St Julian's attracts a more sophisticated crowd.

gregates on the pavement. The ideal spot for relaxing with friends, things certainly liven up as the night goes on.

Hacienda
Baystreet Complex, Level 2, St George's Bay, St Julian's; tel: 7947 0002; Mon–Fri 7pm–4am, Sat–Sun 5pm–4am; map p.135 D2

With a Spanish name meaning 'country home', Hacienda is the bar for party animals after a little Latin flavour. The music is a mix of commercial tunes and live performances by local talent. With friendly

Above: British pubs can still be found if you're missing home.

snacks are super. Huggins has a distinctly British pub feel to it and operates a karaoke stand from Sunday to Friday.

Hugo's Lounge

St Rita's Steps, St George's Road, Paceville; tel: 2138 3639; www.hugosloungemalta.com; daily noon–1am; map p.135 E2

In the centre of Paceville, this is the place to come for great music and an upbeat atmosphere. Sip a mojito or caipirinha while reclining on the comfortable sofas, or take a seat

Malta has become a clubbing venue in its own right, and internationally renowned DJs and performers now include it as part of their tours. For the latest information about who's playing where visit: www.whatson.com.mt.

outside with a bottle of wine or Japanese sake, soaking up the street atmosphere. The upstairs venue gets livelier as the night goes on.

Kloset

Ball Street, Paceville; tel: 7932 4333; www.klozetclub.com; Wed, Fri–Sun from 10pm; map p.135 E2

Despite Malta's strong religious inclinations, Kloset is a club that caters for the gay and lesbian community. It is largely regarded as the premier LGBT venue on the island. Catch a Friday night with the great DJ Kathy-K, 1970s and 1980s music on a Wednesday or the Sunday Latin nights. A guaranteed good time.

Right: the Isle of MTV concert is one of the biggest events in Malta.

Muddywaters

56, Main Street, Balluta Bay, St Julian's; tel: 2137 4155; www.muddywatersbar.net; Mon–Fri noon–late, Sat–Sun 6pm–late; map p.135 E2

Located just outside Paceville, this has been one of the island's most popular nightspots for over 15 years. It is also one of the trendiest rock and blues venues, catering for both younger and older generations. Thursday nights is reserved for live rock music, while Fridays are dedicated to classic rock and blues. With the well-equipped jukebox, it won't be long before you join in with the famous Muddies style of dancing on tables and stools.

Plush Lounge

St George's Road, Paceville; tel: 2738 4300; daily 7.30pm–3am; map p.135 E2

Comprising two rooms, one with a stylish 'L'-

shaped bar, the other a long hall-style expanse softened by red spot lighting, Plush is a great place to go for a bit of fun with a touch of luxury. The extensive cocktail list starts at €3, with Buy One Get One Free tokens continually dispersed outside. The music is a range of chart, R&B and pop, with friendly DJs who are more than happy to play requests. For a quieter experience, there is comfortable wicker seating outside where you can take your drinks or smoke a shish pipe.

Qube – The Vodka Bar
St Rita Road, Paceville; tel: 7935 0680; www.qube malta.com; daily 8.30pm–4am; map p.135 E2
One of Malta's most sought-after bars in the heart of Paceville, Qube is open all week and never fails to draw the liveliest crowds. There are special

Left and right: friendly owners and relaxed bars make up the Malta scene.

themed nights on selected days, top-notch local DJs and unbeatable daily bar offers to create the friendly, fun atmosphere that keeps the crowds coming back night after night.

Ryan's Irish Pub
Spinola Bay, St Julian's; tel: 2135 0680; www.ryans pub.com.mt; daily 5pm–4am; map p.135 E2
The first Irish pub in Malta, Ryan's quickly became a hotspot for locals, tourists

One of the most awaited nights of the annual party calendar is **Isle of MTV**, usually held on the Floriana granaries in July. Like most local events, there is no guarantee that it will happen until it, well, happens, but past performers have included Lady Gaga, the Black Eyed Peas and Maroon 5.

and expatriates thanks to its unique and welcoming atmosphere. There is a full range of foreign and local

95

Left: relaxing on the Waterfront. **Right and below right:** Tattingers.

clubnumerouno.com; Fri 11pm–4am, Sat 11.30pm–4am, Sun 10.30pm–4am; map p.135 C1
With four fully stocked bars and DJs Drew and Ian Lang playing a mix of commercial and R&B, Numero Uno is alive with the energy of thousands of partygoers. On a Saturday there is also a separate space where alternative rock is played in a more chilled-out arena.

Tattingers Club
Telghat Saqqajja, Rabat; tel: 2145 1104; www.tattingers. com; check website for events; map p.134 C1
With a first-class dance floor and VIP area, Tattingers is Malta's first super club and the venue to head to for an unforgettable night. The range of top DJs means that the club oozes energy. 1990s nights run on selected days.

beers at the well-stocked bar, not forgetting the classic Guinness and other stouts. With live local DJs at weekends and the renowned Irish tradition of dancing on tables, this bar is a hub of authentic Celtic activity. It is also one of the island's top sports bars, with events shown live. An extensive menu also caters for those after a quick bar bite.

MDINA AND RABAT
Gianpula
Gianpula Alley, Rabat; tel: 9947 2133; www.gianpula.com; Fri–Sat 10.30pm–4am; map p.134 C1

Established in 1980 and enjoying a 4,000-person capacity, Gianpula is Malta's largest and most renowned open-air club. Comprising three rooms – The Main, Molecule and Groove Gardens, where you can dance and absorb the outdoor atmosphere. The venue has hosted some of the world's top DJs in its time, including Cream and The Ministry of Sound. It has also played host to Malta's biggest open air festivals.

Numero Uno
The Crafts Village, Ta' Qali, Attard; tel: 7949 5694; www.

ST PAUL'S BAY

Amazonia

Dolmen Resort Hotel, Qawra, St
Paul's Bay; tel: 2355 2410;
www.amazoniamalta.com;
daily 10pm–late; map p.134 C3
Chill, dance and relax
while enjoying the very
best that house music has
to offer. Amazonia pio-
neers the freshest new talent, including live
percussion, saxophone
and podium dancers. You
can sit and relax on the
luxury terrace, or dance
with a drink from the bar
until the early hours.

Fuego

Qawra Bay, Qawra, St Paul's
Bay; tel: 2158 4933; www.
fuego.com.mt; free; daily
9pm–4am, Sat–Sun until 6am;
map p.135 C3
Fuego is the only bar on the
island that offers authentic
salsa music with lessons on
selected days. It welcomes
dance- and Latino-lovers
with open arms. In this
uniquely designed venue,

guests can absorb the pure
Latin and commercial music
provided by the top DJs.
Hang out inside to soak up
the lively atmosphere or
step out onto the expansive
open terrace, which is covered and heated during the
cooler months. Foam par-
ties are on Wednesdays
and Fridays from 10pm
onwards.

GOZO

La Grotta Club

Xlendi Road, Xlendi; tel: 2155
1149; seasonally, Sat,
10pm–late; map p.138 B2
Despite the limited
nightlife in Gozo, La
Grotta is one of Europe's
finest outdoor clubs. Situated in Xlendi Valley, the
stunning landscape is a
breathtaking backdrop for
the high-quality sound,
visuals, lasers and lights.
Join the crowds on a Sat-
urday and party until the
early hours, taking the first
ferry back to Malta in the
morning.

Left: Fuego.

97

Pampering

Nothing says relaxation like some time spent being pampered by professionals at a spa, hair salon or nail bar. And the Maltese Islands are teeming with fantastic spots for a little rest and rejuvenation. The majority of the larger hotels now offer some kind of spa facilities, with a variety of beauty and well-being treatments on offer in a range of budgets. Most of the island's spas are centred around Sliema and St Julian's – offering great getaways from the hustle and bustle of this busy region. Treatments vary and are often cheaper than on the continent, but it's recommended to book ahead.

as it was recently refurbished, giving it a new lease of life. Features Malta's first oxygen bar and kinesis rooms, as well as classical facial and body care. Indulge in a 'Mud Scalp Delight' or water lily aromatic bath, and finish things off in the garden relaxation area or enjoy a smoothie by the pool.

SPAS

Atrium Health & Fitness Spa

Hotel Riu Seabank, Marfa Road, Mellieha; tel: 2152 2108; www.atriumspa.com.mt; map p.134 B3

Soak up serenity and soothe sore muscles in the Hotel Riu Seabank. Includes the option of a personal therapist to design your own individual programme and day package. We recommend the 'Ocean's Escape' with Mediterranean salt glow and marine hydro bath.

Corinthia Apollo Day Spa

St George's Bay, St Julian's; tel: 2370 2501; www.corinthia hotels.com; map p.135 E2

Treat yourself at competitive prices with highly qualified and dedicated therapists. Try the treatments on offer for affordable indulgence, from scrubs and wraps to reflexology and facials.

Corinthia Athenaeum Spa

Corinthia Palace Hotel, Vjal De Paule, Balzan; tel: 2144 3001; www.corinthiahotels.com; map p.135 D1

De-stress and restore energy in Corinthia's well-being centre. One of the island's first spas, it is still one of its best, especially

Da Vinci Spa, Pergola Club Hotel & Spa

Triq Adenau, Mellieha; tel: 2152 3912; www.pergolahotel.com.mt/davincispa; map p.134 B3

Experience luxury with wide-ranging treatments. We like the coffee body wrap to firm and trim, or 'Ancient Rituals' like the Hopi ear candle for warmth and inner balance.

Elizir Beauty Salon & Spa

Triq Nutar Debono, Naxxar; tel: 2143 7115; map p.135 D2

With the energy of essen-

Above left: Excelsior Grand Hotel & Spa. **Right:** Fortina Spa Resort.

Left: Atrium Health & Fitness Spa.

Expect professional staff and sophisticated equipment that will soothe your cares away. The space is atmospheric and luxurious, ideal for indulging in a body scrub peeling with marine salts and caviar or chocolate.

Fortina Spa Resort
Tigne Seafront, Sliema; tel: 2346 2346; www.fortinaspa resort.com; map p.135 E2
Malta's best-known spa just seconds from the Sliema commercial district. Four spas and views of Valletta's bastion walls mean relaxation is unavoidable. With over 200 treatments available, a dental clinic and cosmetic surgery, the ways to unwind and boost your inner self are unlimited.

Health & Beauty Fitness Spa
Tigrija Palazz, Level 4, Republic Street, Victoria, Gozo; tel: 2155 3898; www.gozospa.com; map p.132 B2
One of a number of day

Top Treatments:
Spa Sante – Hotel Fortina – **chocolate full body massage.**
Le Spa by Transforma – Maritime Antonine Hotel – **haute couture facials.**
MyoKa Lotus Spa – Le Méridien Hotel – **Mediterranean sea salt body scrub.**
Athenaeum – Corinthia Palace Hotel – **chromoenergetic massage.**
Kempinski Hotel San Lawrenz and Spa – **Balneo bath.**

---

tial oils and deep massages, Elizir offers personalised treatments for slimming, circulation boosting and de-stressing. A great day spa if you're based in this central region.

Excelsior Grand Hotel & Spa
Triq l-Assedju l-Kbir, Floriana; tel: 2319 2115; www.grand excelsiorhotel.com.mt; map p.135 E1

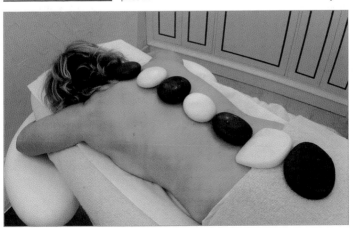

spas popping up in Gozo. This one offers various treatments, including beauty, nails, facials, massages, hydro and algae baths and body wraps. It uses the latest technology such as Rose Aesthetics and intense pulsed light for permanent hair removal.

Kempinski Hotel San Lawrenz
San Lawrenz, Gozo; tel: 2211 5210; www.kempinski-gozo.com; map p.138 A3

Gozo's best-known spa is a haven in stunning natural surroundings. Book yourself in for as long as you can to focus on eliminating toxins and to balance body, mind and soul. Offers an array of treatments including Ayurveda, marine and herbal care, massages, Balneo baths and Vichy water showers.

Lotus Spa and Health
39, Main Street, Balluta Bay, St Julian's; tel: 2311 2360; www.lemeridien.com/myokaspa; map p.135 E2

A true escape from the

bustling St Julian's world outside. This is a world of water, warmth and well-being, and all treatments concentrate on cleansing and energy restoration. Escape everyday life with complimentary advice for both men and women, and individually targeted packages.

Radisson SAS Golden Sands Resort & Spa
Golden Bay, l/o Mellieha; tel: 2356 1000; www.goldensands.com.mt; map p.134 B3

A refreshing and recommended break for men, women, teenagers and

mums-to-be. This spa offers 80 holistic, oriental, de-stressing, anti-ageing and rejuvenating treatments in wonderful surroundings.

San Antonio Hotel & Spa
Triq it-Turisti, Qawra, St Paul's Bay; tel: 2158 3434; www.sanantonio-malta.com; map p.134 C3

This centre for relaxation comprises the Le Marquis Spa and the New Form Fitness Centre. Opt for classic treatments that include waxing, facials and manicures or try the popular chocolate massage or the island's only ice grotto.

Spa Du Soleil
Ramla Bay Resort, Marfa, Mellieha; tel: 2281 2281; map p.134 A4

Lots of natural light and secluded views of Gozo and Comino are core to the tranquil atmosphere at Spa du Soleil. Make use of

the whirlpool, sauna and Jacuzzi, steam and massage rooms and beauty treatments for the ultimate in relaxation.

Ta' Cenc Wellness Spa
Hotel Ta' Cenc, Triq Ta' Cenc, Sannat, Gozo; tel: 2219 1600; map p.138 B2
Built on Calypso Island's highest point and overlooking stunning cliffs, 'the last paradise' of Ta' Cenc is perfect to pamper and soothe yourself. Includes packages such as combined spa and lunch and the island's only indoor/outdoor pool.

HAIRDRESSERS, BEAUTY AND NAILS
Arete'
3 Wileg Street, Qawra; tel: 2157 9569; map p.135 C3
Greek for 'virtue' or 'being the best you can be', the renowned Adam Lam created Arete' from his experience in America, Europe and Asia. Comprises three areas: the beauty therapy

room, the nail and manicure station and the haircare area. Make-up and makeovers are also available.

Aura Ltd
Shop 2, Alborada Apts, Triq il-Kbira, Sliema; tel: 2132 4895; www.nailcrazy.com; map p.135 E2
Nail specialists that will give your fingers that finished look. Products used include Minx – the ultimate 'bling' for nails.

Heaven Salon
Tigne Seafront, Sliema; tel: 2346 1001; www.been2 heaven.co.uk; map p.135 E2
Headed by a top London stylist and with creations that have featured on catwalks, you can relax on a Shiatsu backwash chair for a head massage, knowing that your hair will be well looked after.

L'Orchidee
Triq il-Qroll, Bugibba; tel: 2158 2228; map p.134 C3
A luxurious hair and beauty salon in the heart

of Bugibba. Pamper yourself at reasonable prices with personalised treatments and in a relaxing atmosphere. Rid yourself of those puffy legs and feet with the one-and-a-half-hour 'My Aching Feet' treatment for only €30.

Toni & Guy
247–249 Rue D'Argens, Gzira; tel: 2131 0020; www.toniandguy.com.mt; map p.135 D2
This renowned hair brand was brought to Malta by London artistic director Gordon Mayo, who handpicked the salon's talent. As a customer of these fashion and TV stylists, expect to feel stylish and glamorous when you leave.

Victoire Hair & Nails
J.F. Marks Street, San Gwann; tel: 2137 8205; map p.135 D2
A one-stop session without any hassle will transform your hair. Creativity lies in the stylist's interest in fashion, and you can indulge in the nail bar while you wait for your appointment.

Left: Lotus Spa and Health.

Parks and Gardens

Vegetation-lovers may be instantly disappointed to note that the Maltese Islands lack a certain luscious green tinge, especially during the summer months when most flora dries to a crisp. But while large and expansive gardens certainly aren't in plentiful supply, the ones the islands do have make up for it with rich historical and cultural content and, often, breathtaking views. Valletta is something of a hotspot for beautiful gardens, many of which were recently made over, blending old-style decor with exotic plant life and plenty of space to sit and people-watch.

Argotti Botanical Gardens
Floriana; daily 7am–6pm; map p.135 E1
Originally intended as the private garden for Grand Master Pinto in the 18th century, Argotti became a botanical garden around a century later. Highlights include the variety of water features, rich collection of plant and cacti, and the wonderful gazebo which dates back to 1741.

Buskett Gardens
Rabat; map p.134 C1
The perfect picnic spot, these rich gardens were originally planted by the Knights of St John as a hunting spot. Today home to vineyards, Mediterranean pines, olive and lemon groves, it is also the venue for the vibrant *L'Imnarja* folklore festival held each summer.

Garden of Rest
Floriana; Tue, Thur, Sat and first Sun of the month 9.30am–noon; www.dinlarthelwa.org; map p.135 E1
This bastion garden served as a Protestant cemetery from 1806–56 and was recently restored to its former glory. Peaceful and pretty, with great views.

Gardjola Gardens
Senglea; daily 9.30am–10pm; map p.135 E1
Perched on the bastions with panoramic views over the Grand Harbour and Valletta, this garden was originally planned by Grand Master de la Sengle in 1551. Not particularly green, it is home to several mature palms and ficus, and makes a wonderful sunset spot.

Hasting's Garden
Valletta; daily 7am–9pm; map p.132 A1
If you're in Valletta it's worth popping into these recently renovated gardens. Named after a former governor general, the Marquess of Hasting, these sizeable gardens also enjoy stunning views of Manoel Island and Msida Creek.

Howard Gardens
Mdina; map p.134 C1
These are probably the largest public gardens in Malta, forming a natural boundary between Rabat

Left and below left: the gardens at Palazzo Parisio.

eral generations. Open to the public since 1882, enjoy its cobbled walkways, families of ducks and swans swimming in ornamental ponds and the beautiful sculptures and aviary.

Ta' Qali National Park
Ta' Qali; map p.135 C1
An open space ideal for picnics. Not particularly attractive or lush, but a great space for children to run around. Regeneration works are ongoing.

Upper Barrakka Gardens
Valletta; daily winter 7am–9pm, summer 7am–11pm; map p.132 B1
Seconds' walk from Auberge de Castille et Leon, these beautiful gardens are a haven in the city. With incredible views of the Grand Harbour and Three Cities, the paths are lined with busts, statues and plaques that chart various personalities and other significant events in Maltese history.

The **national plant** is the evergreen Maltese Rock-Century with its beautiful magenta-coloured flowerheads. Grown only in Malta and Gozo, it is far from abundant but can be spotted on country walks along the cliffs.

and neighbouring Mdina. Named after Malta's first prime minister, they were made public in 1924 and still remain popular today.

Independence Gardens
Tower Road, Sliema; map p.135 E2
Paved and pretty, this is one of the most popular public gardens. A small play area makes it a favourite with families.

Palazzo Parisio
Victory Square, Naxxar; tel: 2141 2461; www.palazzo parisio.com; daily 9am–6pm with exceptions, last admission 4.30pm; charge; map p.135 D2
A mêlée of colour and scents, this is one of

Malta's most spectacular gardens. Walled and with a mixture of symmetry with many Mediterranean and exotic species.
SEE ALSO MUSEUMS, P.87

San Anton Gardens
Attard; daily 8am–7pm with exceptions; map p.135 D1
San Anton Gardens are regarded as a fine gem among Maltese gardens and have delighted locals and tourists alike over sev-

Right: San Anton Gardens.

Restaurants

Food here is serious business, and locals will travel the length and breadth of the island to get to a restaurant they love. Avoid pricey tourist traps that tend to offer crowd-pleasers instead of more genuine fare, and be prepared sometimes to dig a little deeper than the crowded city eateries that are the easiest to stumble across. While St Julian's has long been the obvious choice for good food, the north is now making a name for itself, with fantastic offerings mushrooming across the region. If you're looking for the freshest and best local ingredients, don't miss a trip over to Gozo.

VALLETTA

Ambrosia
137, Archbishop's Street, Valletta; tel: 2122 5923; Mon–Sat 12.30–2.30pm, Tue–Sat 7.30–10pm; $$; map p. 132 C3
Chef patron Chris has built several restaurants from the ground up, and this is his masterpiece that stood the test of time. A black chalkboard boasts the daily-changing menu, while certain staples – including a delicious cheese soufflé and Gozo asparagus salad – ensure foodies return again and again.

Blue Room
59, Republic Street, Valletta; tel: 2123 8014; Tue–Fri, Sun noon–2.30pm, daily 7–11pm; $$$; map p.132 B2
Top Chinese cuisine in the heart of the city, Blue Room is a hip mix of mod-

Above: pastizzerias like Max serve delicious local *pastizzi* filled with savoury cheese and aromatics.

ern decor and traditional cooking. Despite the fact that it is far pricier than other oriental restaurants, locals flock to it for its faultless food and favourites that include baked satay chicken and crispy Peking duck served with pancakes.

The Carriage
22/5, Valletta Buildings, South Street, Valletta; tel: 2124 7828; Tue–Fri 12.30–2.30pm, Thur–Sat 7.30–10pm; $$; map p.132 A2

This is one of the city's stalwarts, with spectacular sea and rooftop views from its splendid open-air terrace. Known for its gourmet touches and innovative cuisine.

Cockney's
Il-Moll Ta Marsamxett, Valletta; tel: 2123 6065; daily 12.30–2.30pm, Tue–Sun 7–10pm; $$; map p.132 B4
A little off the beaten track but worth the trek down to the Valletta coast. Alternatively take the ferry across from Sliema as it berths seconds away from this delicious fish eatery. Trust the fresh fish of the day, grilled to perfection, or the sumptuous selection of fried seafood.

Da Pippo Trattoria
136, Triq Melita, Valletta; tel: 2124 8029; Mon–Sat noon–3.30pm; $; map p.132 B2
Often voted Valletta's best budget restaurant, this rustic Mediterranean trattoria is loved by city businessmen who flock here for lazy Friday lunches. Home-

Prices for an average two-course meal with half a bottle of house wine:
€ under €20
€€ €20–€40
€€€ over €20

Left: St Julian's Barracuda.

you if you don't like garlic, but is unmissable if you're hoping to unearth a true taste of the city.

Malata

St George's Square, Valletta: tel: 2123 3967; Mon–Sat noon–2.30pm and 7–11pm; $$; map p.132 B3

Buried beneath the recently renovated St George's Square, just seconds' walk from Republic Street, this stylish restaurant offers the best in French-Mediterranean cuisine. Family-run, so expect superb hospitality, wonderful food and a good wine list.

Trattoria Palazz

43, Old Theatre Street, Valletta; tel: 2122 6611; Mon–Sat 12.30–2.30pm and 7.30–10pm; $$; map p.132 B3

What used to be a palace cellar is now a hotspot for good Italian and Mediterranean food and great fish dishes. Run by a local family; enjoy the intimate setting below the National Library.

SLIEMA, ST JULIAN'S & PACEVILLE

Barracuda

194/195 Triq il-Kbira, St Julian's; tel: 2133 1817;

Malta's national dish is **rabbit**, usually marinated overnight in wine and fried in plenty of garlic. It is more of an event than just a meal, and locals love to head to small town restaurants for a *fenkata* (which usually kicks off with spaghetti in a rich rabbit sauce, and is followed by the real deal served in a very casual manner with chips and salad). We can recommend the finger-licking food served up by Ta Soldi in Mgarr (tel: 2152 5815; daily D).

---

cooked, fresh food is the speciality, and it's fun to share from the large pans of different pastas placed on the table. Always packed, so booking is essential.

Fumia

Old Bakery Street, Valletta; tel: 21317053; Tue–Sun 12.30–2.30 and 8–10.30; $$$; map p.132 C3

Set under the Manoel Theatre, this is a cosy and intimate restaurant offering some of the best fish on

the island. It is run by a Sicilian family, and you can bank on genuine food cooked to perfection – but it's best to check the prices of the fresh catch before you buy, because prices can soar.

King's Own Band Club

Republic Street, Valletta; tel: 2123 0281; daily noon–10.30pm, $; map p.132 B2

Great, traditional food, a casual atmosphere and fantastic value. The headquarters of a popular Valletta band club is now also a convenient but delicious stop for a spot of wonderful food. This one's not for

Above: vintage advert.

6.30–11pm daily; $$$; map p.135 D2
Past guests have included Madonna and Claudia Schiffer, so dress to impress at this fine dining, seafront restaurant. Centrally located but still intimate and exclusive, gastronomic specialities are in abundance and satisfaction is pretty much guaranteed. Booking is essential, especially if you want a table on the terrace.

Bianco's
21, St George's Road, St Julian's; tel: 2135 9865; daily noon–2.30pm and 7–11pm; $; map p.135 D2

Prices for an average two-course meal with half a bottle of house wine:
€ under €20
€€ €20–€40
€€€ over €20

The decor is delightfully chic but the atmosphere is relaxed. Expect young, friendly staff and an abundant menu that offers something for everyone, from grills and pasta to pizza, platters and salads. Centrally located, just minutes' walk from the Paceville entertainment district.

Blue Elephant
Hilton Hotel, St Julian's; tel: 2138 3383; daily 7–11pm; $$$; map p.135 D2
A franchise and perfect culinary concept combined in an unmatched ambience. Thai food at its best served in stunning surroundings that include a waterfall and lush vegetation. Pricey, but worth it.

Bouzouki
35 Triq Spinola, St Julian's; tel: 2138 7127; daily 7–10pm; $$;

Right: fish and pasta make up much of Maltese cuisine.

map p.135 D2
Malta's best Greek restaurant, with all the delicious bits you'd expect, including dips, fried feta cheese, moresh warm bread and kebabs. Overlooking Spinola Bay, with outdoor tables by the seafront during the summer months.

La Cuccagna
47, Triq Ameri, Sliema; tel: 2134 6703; Tue–Sun 7pm–midnight; $; map p.135 E2
Great food at reasonable prices and just off the Sliema promenade. Recently expanded, but still run by the same friendly and formidable team, La Cuccagna specialises in delicious pizza, pasta and grills.

Garam Masalaa
11, The Strand, Ta Xbiex, Msida; tel: 9902 1882; Tue–Sat 7pm–10pm, Sun 12.30–2.30pm; $; map p.135 E1
Ignore the less than enticing decor and enjoy the authentic Indian cuisine

rustled up by this delightful husband-and-wife team. Superb specialities include their creamy korma and crispy samosas.

Henry J Beans
Corinthia Hotel St George's, Il-Bajja Ta San Gorg; tel: 2370 2694; daily noon–3pm and 7–11pm; $; map p.135 E2
This franchise has become a staple, and locals love its frivolous mix of American favourites and yummy cocktails. Dine on the expansive terrace during the summer months, or enjoy the eclectic decor indoors.

Hugo's Tapas
St George's Bay, St Julian's; tel: 2138 3634; daily noon–2.30pm and 7–11pm; $$; map p.135 E2
A relatively new kid on the block but one that has made its mark. Seconds' walk from Paceville; enjoy the chic, Spanish-inspired decor and the tapas menu that includes daily specials and sumptuous desserts.

Left: basic ingredients for a rustic cuisine. **Right:** St Julian's Piccolo Padre *(see p.108)*.

Honey is a staple of many Maltese dishes, and most restaurateurs prefer to stay true to the local versions. In fact, the Maltese Islands have long been known for their spicy-sweet honey, prompting the Greeks and Romans to nickname them *Melita* (honey). Today you can purchase plenty of different varieties to take back home in pretty jars but keep your eyes especially peeled for those infused with wild thyme, citrus and carob.

Krishna Indian Cuisine
97, The Strand, Sliema; tel: 2134 6291; daily 7–10pm, Sun 12.30–2.30pm; $$; map p.135 E2
Known for being one of the first Indian restaurants on the island, this place has stood the test of time. The decor here changes regularly, and specialities include the delicious chicken tikka masala and nutty lamb korma.

Paranga
Intercontinental Malta, St George's Bay, St Julian's; tel: 21377600; daily noon–3pm and 7–11pm; $$$; map p.135 E2

A beautiful spot to wine and dine, you literally couldn't get any closer to the sea without falling in. Overlooking St George's Bay; enjoy a delightful mix of fresh pasta dishes, meats and grilled fish strongly influenced by Sicilian flavours.

Peppinos
31 Triq San Gorg, Paceville; tel: 2137 3200; Mon–Sat noon–2.30pm and 7–11pm; $$; map p.135 E2
A true favourite and an eatery that has attracted celebs including Brad Pitt and Bon Jovi in his time. The exceptional food is a mix of Mediterranean

Above: Cisk is the local beer.

flavours including pasta, salads and meat that is always cooked to perfection.

Piccolo Padre
194–195 Triq il-Kbira, St Julian's; tel: 2134 4875; daily 6.30–11.30pm, Sun 12.30–3pm; $; map p.135 D2
A fun and atmospheric pizza and pasta joint that is always bustling. Perfect for families, the menu never fails to delight, and favourites include their delicious closed pizza stuffed with gorgonzola cheese and honey. A great selection of gluten-free and healthy dishes is also available.

The huge majority of local restaurants will provide complimentary bread and crackers at the start of your meal. Some even serve a little appetiser to whet your appetite. One to look out for is *bigilla*, a not particularly attractive-looking (but extremely tasty) dip made from beans and plenty of garlic. It is usually served with *galletti* – bite-sized water biscuits.

Snoopy's
3, Main Street, St Julian's; tel: 2134 5466; Sat–Sun noon–3pm, Wed–Mon 6.30–11pm; $$; map p.135 D2
Run by sisters who really know their thing, Snoopy's is best known for its meat (cooked to perfection) and Mediterranean-oriental fusion food. Dine upstairs and enjoy a pre/post-dinner cocktail in the bar downstairs.

Ta' Kris
Fawwara Lane, off Bisazza Street, Sliema; tel: 2133 7367; daily 12.30–3.30pm and 6.30–11.30pm; $; map p.135 E2
Great home cooking in the heart of the island's commercial district, Ta' Kris is found down a side alley, so keep your eyes peeled for it. Superb pasta and Maltese-style cuisine in a relaxed atmosphere.

Tana Del Lupo
58a/b Triq il-Wilga, St Julian's tel: 2135 3294; Tue–Sun 12.30–2.30pm, Mon–Sat 7.30–10.45pm; $$$; map p.135 D2
Paceville may not be known for its restaurants, but this is the exception to the rule. Wonderful fish and meat dishes, cooked to the Sicilian owner's high standards. Bit on the pricey side, especially for fish.

Vecchia Napoli
255, Tower Road, Sliema; daily noon–2.30pm and 6.30–11pm; $; map p.135 E2
Booking is absolutely essential at this fresh pizza/pasta joint that has made quite a stir. Locals love its ample portions and impeccable quality; don't miss the caprese salad with oozing buffalo mozzarella and its speciality closed pizza.

Zen Japanese Cuisine

Portomaso, St Julian's; tel: 2138 6500; Tue–Sun 7.30–10pm; $$$, map p.135 D2
Definitely one of the best sushi restaurants on the island, served by knowledgeable staff and in beautiful surroundings. The set menu, which includes miso soup, sushi and green-tea ice cream, isn't cheap but is still good value.

Zeri's

Portomaso Marina, Portomaso, St Julian's; tel: 2135 9559; Sun noon–2.30pm (winter only), daily 7–11pm; $$$; map p.135 D2
Consistently good food that never fails to satisfy, the team behind Zeri's know their stuff. Meat- and fish-lovers will be spoilt for choice, and there is also a good choice of vegetarian fare.

Left: rabbit is Malta's national dish.

Zest

12, St George's Road, St Julian's; tel: 2138 7600; Mon–Sat 7–11pm; $$$; map p.135 D2
Within Malta's only boutique hotel, this is the spot where East meets West and fantastic cuisine is found. An innovative menu and striking, contemporary decor in the heart of Spinola Bay.

RABAT, MDINA & DINGLI

Bacchus

1, Triq Inguanez, Mdina: tel: 2145 4489; daily noon–3.30pm and 7–11pm; $$$; map p.134 C1
Hidden down one of Mdina's picturesque alleys, Bacchus has long been the restaurant of choice for those after something a little bit special. Intimate and romantic, there is also an excellent wine list to choose from.

Bobbyland

Triq Panoramica, Dingli Cliffs, Dingli; tel: 2145 2895; Tue–Sun 12.30–2.30pm, Tue–Sat 7–10.30pm; $; map p.136 A2
A little off the beaten track on the Dingli Cliffs, Bobbyland overlooks the

Mediterranean Sea and is a true, relaxed taste of Malta. Specialities include the traditional rabbit in garlic, as well as numerous pasta dishes.

De Mondion

Misrah il-Kunsill, Mdina; tel: 2145 0560; Mon–Sat 7.30–

Feeling a bit peckish but not quite ready for a full meal? Locals love *hobz biz-zejt*, a refreshing snack made from crusty bread filled with tomatoes, capers, olives, beans and lashings of olive oil that really hits the spot. Most roadside cafés will sell this delight, but Andrew's Bar (St Antony's Road, Birkirkara; tel: 2149 1222) is definitely the best.

Pick of the Best
By the Sea
Paranga, Kartell
Mediterranean
Vecchia Napoli, Peppinos
Maltese
Tatitas, Ta Maria
Fish
Rizzu, Fumia
Oriental
Blue Elephant, Blue Room
Something Special
De Mondion, Ta Frenc

109

Above: catch of the day.

10.30pm; $$$; map p.134 C1
With panoramic views from the Mdina Bastions, this truly is one of the most exclusive spots to eat on the island and prices certainly reflect that. Their dishes are tantalising and unique, and if you're in the mood for something special opt for the sumptuous tasting menu combining all of the chef's best dishes.

Medina
7, Triq is-Salib Imqaddes, Mdina; tel: 2145 4004; Mon–Sat 7.30–10pm; $$; map p.134 C1
Dine on modern Mediterranean cuisine in truly romantic surroundings

beneath the flowering oleander tree in the vine-clustered courtyard during the summer, and by an open log fireplace during the winter months.

THE CENTRE
Lord Nelson
Triq il-Kbira, Mosta; tel: 2143 2590; Tue–Sat 7.30–10.30pm with exceptions; $$; map p.135 C2
Book ahead to secure the delightful table on the tiny balcony overlooking the Mosta Dome in one of the town's oldest buildings. The food here is excellent, although quite pricey, and the ambience is welcoming and intimate.

Luna di Sera
Palazzo Parisio, Victory Square, Naxxar: tel: 2141 2461; Wed–Sat 7–11.30pm; $$$; map p.135 D2
Fine dining in Malta came of age with the opening of Luna di Sera. Located within a centuries-old palazzo; guests have been wooed by the exciting menu, wonderful wine list and special table set-up

Right: Mirabelle's casual setting.

with crystal, fine china, silver and candles.
SEE ALSO MUSEUMS, P.87

Ta' Maria
Triq il-Kostituzzjoni, Mosta; tel: 2143 4444; daily noon–2.30pm and 6.30–11.30pm; $$; map p.135 C2
One of the most authentic tastes of Malta, this bustling eatery has consistently been voted the Best Maltese Food Restaurant on the island. Traditional and fresh fare is the order of the day, and entertainment (such as folklore dancing) is in abundance.

BAHAR IC-CAGHAQ, BUGIBBA AND ST PAUL'S BAY
Mirabelle's
Bay Square, Bugibba; tel: 2157 2163; daily noon–3pm and 6.30–11pm; $; map p.134 C3
Within easy reach of the promenade, Mirabelle's is the best of a bunch of casual pub-style eateries along this road. Beloved by its (largely) British clientele,

R

110

the food is good and the atmosphere always electric.

Ta' Cassia
Triq il-Katakombi, Salina, l/o Bugibba; tel: 2157 1431; daily 7.30–10pm, Sun 12.30–3pm; $$; map p.1315 C3
Situated in a 180-year-old house of character and overlooking the Salina salt-pans, there's a sense of tranquillity at Ta' Cassia. The food is a delicious mix of Maltese and international dishes and the service attentive.

THE SOUTH
Grabiel
Misrah Mifsud Bonnici, Marsascala; tel: 2163 4194; daily noon–2.30pm and 7–10pm; $$; map p.137 E2
A favourite for fish lovers, Grabiel is one of the restaurants locals are prepared to cross the island to get to. Trust the fish to be some of the freshest on the island.

Ir-Rizzu
52, Xatt is-Sajjieda, Marsaxlokk; tel: 2165 1569;

Left: the classy Medina restaurant. **Right:** Maltese capers.

Prices for an average two-course meal with half a bottle of house wine:
€ under €20
€€ €20–€40
€€€ over €20

---

daily noon–2.30pm and 7–10.30pm; $$; map p.137 E2
A beloved eatery just off the Marsaxlokk seafront. If you only go to one fish restaurant, make this it, and be sure to opt for the seafood platter which includes octopus, mussels, calamari and giant prawns.

Southport Villa and Gardens
91, Xatt is-Sajjieda, Marsaxlokk; tel: 2701 2600; daily noon–3pm and 7–10.30pm; $$; map p.137 E2
One of the most exclusive eateries in this part of the island, Southport is something of a haven off the busy seafront. Leondardo, upstairs, is the gourmet section, while downstairs and in the beautiful gardens dining is a little more relaxed but still excellent.

THE NORTH
The Arches
113, Triq Gorg Borg Olivier, Mellieha; tel: 2152 3460; Mon–Sat 7–10.30pm; $$$; map p.134 B3
Another of the island's best, The Arches has been going for years and is the sort of place that seems to get better with age. Intimate and cosy, with delicious fare and an expansive wine cellar to explore.

Giuseppe's
Main Street, Mellieha; tel: 2157 4882; Mon–Sat 7.30–10.30pm; $$; map p.134 B3
A real find in the heart of picturesque Mellieha. Giuseppe's is run by local foodie family the Dian-

conos, so you can expect excellent and innovative food made from the freshest local ingredients.

Palazzo Santa Rosa

Triq il-Mistra, St Paul's Bay; tel: 2158 2737; Tue–Sun; Tue–Sun 12.30–3pm and 7.30–10.30pm; $$$; map p.134 C3

A truly outstanding gastronomic experience. Using only the freshest ingredients (most of which are grown in the surrounding organic fields), Palazzo Santa Rosa redefines modern-traditional cuisine to come up with delicious slow-cooked food. Any wait is well worth it – a must for all gastronomes.

GOZO
Kartell

Triq il-Port, Marsalforn; tel: 2155 6918; daily 11.30am–3pm and 6.30–10.30pm; $$; map p.138 C4

Right on the water's edge, you'll need to book ahead to beat the hordes of Maltese who travel to Gozo just for a fish meal at Kartell. Opt for the catch of the day, grilled to perfection.

Maldonado Bistro

8, Assumption Street, Victoria; tel: 2701 9270; Tue–Sun 12.30–2.30pm and 7–11pm; $; map p.138 B3

The perfect spot for lunch if you're hoping to avoid the crowds, Maldonado offers super grills, pasta and salad dishes in beautiful surroundings.

Oleander

10, Pjazza Vittorio, Xaghra; tel: 2155 7230; Tue–Sun noon–3pm and 7–10.30pm; $$; map p.139 C3

One of the favourites on Gozo, Oleander is set in a pretty Xaghra square and you can soak up plenty of atmosphere while dining here. Great food, including pasta, meat and traditional local delicacies, and an

Prices for an average two-course meal with half a bottle of house wine:
€ under €20
€€ €20–€40
€€€ over €20

Above and right: Ta' Frenc.

extensive wine list.

Otters

Triq Santa Marija, Marsalforn; tel: 2156 2473; daily noon–4pm and 7–11pm; $$; map p.138 C4

Another spot for lovers of the sea. The food here is a pleasant mix of grills, pasta and salad dishes, and the night time ambience out on the large terrace is second to none.

Ta' Frenc

Triq Marsalforn, Marsalforn; tel: 2155 3888; Wed–Mon 7–10pm; $$$; map p.138 C4

Widely regarded as the best restaurant in the Maltese Islands, Ta' Frenc has

a host of awards under its belt, and for good reason. Only the best ingredients make it, and the result is a gastronomic explosion of flavours. The latest addition is the chef's luxury five-course menu which, although pricey, is certainly worth a try. Perfect for any special occasion.

Ta' Rikardu

4, Triq il-Fosos, Citadella, Victoria; tel: 2155 5953; daily until 7pm; $; map p.138 B3
The spot for genuine local fare, lunch at Ta' Rikardu is fun and flavoursome. Far from gourmet, expect a platter of Gozo cheese, olives, capers, fresh tomatoes and the most addictive bread you could imagine.

Tatitas

Pjazza San Lawrenz, San Lawrenz; tel: 2156 6482; 1 March–end October, daily noon–2.30pm and 7–10.30pm; $$; map p.138 A3
Dine in the picturesque

San Lawrenz Square and enjoy the hospitality of the charming couple who run this traditional eatery. The food is always good and full of local flavours. Favourites include the baby lobster risotto, ravioli, rabbit and beef olives.

Tmun Victoria

Triq L-Ewropa, Victoria; tel: 2156 6667; Fri–Wed 6.30–10.30pm, Sun noon–2.30pm; $$; map p.138 B3
The perfect blend of upmarket food in a comfortable atmosphere. Known for their fish dishes, the extensive menu also includes some of the best meat on the island and desserts that are worth waiting for.

Left: Gozo's promenade.
Right: homemade preserves.

Shopping

With very few indigenous shops, Malta is often regarded as one of Europe's poorer shopping destinations, especially as imported goods are usually more expensive here than back home. But don't disregard it – the commercial centre Sliema does have a reasonable selection of internationally known shops, dotted through malls or around Bisazza Street and The Strand. You'll find more independent outlets in Valletta, including those selling shoes, leather, clothing and silver and gold jewellery. If it's authentic, local souvenirs and crafts that you want, try the Ta' Qali Craft Centre for a variety of locally blown glass, filigree and pottery.

MADE IN MALTA

Denis Filigree Works

Hut 77, Ta' Qali Crafts Village, Attard; tel: 2143 0926; times vary; map p.135 C1
Maltese filigree is famous the world over, and this little establishment is the spot to watch it being made and to purchase fine examples of it. The range includes traditional styles, such as the Maltese Cross, as well as more modern varieties.

Mdina Glass

Ta' Qali Crafts Centre; tel: 2141 5786; www.mdina glass.net; daily 10am–10pm; map p.135 C1
This family-run business is something of a local institution. View the glistening displays of hand-made glass that characterise the silent city. Watch the glass-blowers as they work in stiflingly hot conditions, then nip into the air-conditioned shop to buy everything from dinner sets to photo frames and vases to Christmas dec-

Above: Maltese embroidery.

orations. There is also a small collection of delightful glass jewellery.

Ta Dbiegi Crafts Centre

Frangisk Portelli Street, San Lawrenz, Gozo; June–Sept 9.30am–6pm, Oct–May 9.30am–4.30pm; map p.138 A3
Situated between Gharb and San Lawrenz, this is Gozo's only craft centre. While away some time watching the craftsmen at work as they skilfully create their goods before moving on to purchase a souvenir in the on-site shop.

MALLS AND COMPLEXES

Arkadia Commercial Centre

Fortunato Mizzi Street, Victoria, Gozo; tel: 2210 3000; www. arkadia.com.mt; July–Sept 9am–7pm, Oct–June 9am– 1pm, 4–7pm; map p.138 B2
A bustling contemporary centre, the Arkadia provided Gozo with its first mall. Comprises a large department store featuring international clothing and homeware brands, as well as a basement food store that is renowned for its fresh produce. It combines choice, quality and value for money.

Baystreet Complex

St George's Bay, St Julian's; tel: 2138 4422; www.baystreet. com.mt; daily 10am–10pm; map p.135 E2
Baystreet was the first complex to introduce Sunday shopping to the islands. This is the largest shopping complex in Malta and home to renowned brands including Mexx,

Left: shopping in Sliema.

beauty, lifestyle and food, nestled between the cafés and shops in the heart of Sliema's commercial district. Compromises several floors of quality retailing built around a central hall. Brands includes Benetton, Miss Selfridge and Promod.

FASHION

Accessorize & Monsoon

2–3 Bisazza Street, Sliema; tel: 2131 7951; Mon–Fri 9.30am–7pm, Sat 9.30am–7.30pm; map p.135 E2

Offers a beautiful collection of clothing and various styles of accessories. The exciting range includes fashion for women and children and accessories that take you from day into evening, including bags, wallets, flip-flops and costume jewellery.

De Fort Designwear

15, Portomaso, St Julian's; tel: 2138 7687; daily 9am–7pm; map p.135 D2

Backing onto the marina, this is the spot to find big-name clothing brands for men and women. Stocks day and evening wear, swimwear and accessories with brands including Lacoste, Polo Jeans and Timberland.

Diesel

222, Merchants Street, Valletta; tel: 2258 4443; June–Aug Mon–Sat 10am–7.30pm, Sept–May Mon–Sat 9.30am–2pm, 4–7pm; map p.132 B1

Renowned for Italian jeans and casuals. Shop for casual and evening wear, shoes and accessories for

Everybody loves a good market, and the **Valletta Sunday Market**, held a minute's walk from the main bus terminus, is plenty of fun. Dig through the tat to find the odd bargain, or just enjoy the lively atmosphere.

French Connection and Guess. There's a bookshop on Level One, which stocks a fantastic selection of books and international magazines.

Duke Mall

Victoria, Gozo; July–Sept Mon–Thur 9am–7pm, Fri–Sat 9am–8pm, Oct–June Mon–Thur 9am–1pm, 4–7pm, Fri 9am–1pm, 4–8pm, Sat 9am–8pm; map p.138 B3

Formerly the Duke of Edinburgh Hotel and situated adjacent to the pretty Villa Rundle Gardens in Victoria, the Duke Mall is the new kid on an increasingly commercial block. Features UPIM, TipTop and Accessorize, as well as a food store and day spa.

Embassy Complex

St Lucy's Street, Valletta; tel: 2122 7436; www.embassy complex.com.mt; Mon–Sat 9am–1pm, 4–7pm; map p.132 B2

The capital's leading shopping centre combined with a cinema complex and bingo hall. Encompasses most big fashion and beauty brands, digital and TV services and a lotto booth.

Plaza Shopping Centre

Bisazza Street, Sliema; tel: 2134 3832; www.plaza-shopping.com; Mon–Sat 9am–1pm, 4–7pm; map p.135 E2

The centre for fashion,

Left: Plaza Shopping Centre.

Fruit and vegetables can be expensive when bought from supermarkets, so take a leaf out of the locals' book and source a great produce van instead *(see right)*. Most villages will have one or two of these trucks swinging round their way each morning, and you can be sure that the fruit and veg bought here will be far superior to what you get in the shops; just watch the price and always ask the cost before buying.

both men and women, with the latest collections featuring intimate lines, bags, accessories and footwear.

Kenjo & Kyoto
128 and 52 Old Theatre Street, Valletta; tel: 2122 0724; Mon–Sat 9am–1pm, 4–7pm; map p.132 B3
The spot for elegant, smart styles and stunning quality. Perfect if you need a last-minute dress that transforms you into the belle of the ball.

Marks & Spencer
53–54 Strait Street, Valletta; tel: 2122 0614; Mon–Sat 9am–7pm; map p.133 C3
The British chain has long been a local staple loved by all. Stocking clothing, gifts and now a range of fresh and frozen foods, Marks & Spencer is convenient and well priced.

Max Mara
46 Tower Road, Sliema; tel: 2134 1961; Mon–Sat 9.30am–1pm, 4–7pm; map.135 E2
Found in the major retail centre of Sliema, among the café life and bustling shoppers, Max Mara stocks top name brands with latest-season trends and catwalk-inspired items.

Nara Camicie
1, Bisazza Street, Sliema; tel: 2133 2587; Mon–Sat 9.30am–7.30pm; map p.135 E2
Renowned outlet for some of the most original shirts money can buy. Admittedly on the expensive side, this store only ever stocks one size of each style at any one time, ensuring you stay original.

Rebelli
Church Street, Portomaso, St Julian's; tel: 2138 4050;

www.rebelli.com; Mon–Sat 10am–1pm, 3–8pm, Sun 4–8pm; map p.135 D2
Spread over three stories, many happy hours have been spent hurling cash at the posh brands on offer here. One of the most upmarket outlets in Malta, this is the place to splash out on quality clothes, shoes, bags and accessories.

Shu
St Lucy's Street, Valletta; tel: 2122 8182; Mon–Sat 9.30am–1.30pm, 4–7pm; map.138 B2
An inviting shop stocking sexy shoes. Brands include Sixty and Firetrap for men, and Miss Sixty and Killah for women. Also stocks Fornarina and Guess shoes and accessories.

Solaris
281, Republic Street, Valletta; tel: 2123 2955; Mon–Sat 9.30am–7pm; map p.133 C3
A leading boutique dedicated to designer sunglasses and a trendsetter

for must-have styles. Solaris fashion has featured on catwalks in Dubai fashion week, with its mêlée of modern elegance and radical shapes to suit all tastes.

Zara
1, Tower Road, Sliema; tel: 2131 7951; Mon–Sat 9.30am–7.30pm; map.135 E2
This Spanish fashion sensation draws the crowds, so be prepared to jostle for that must-have jumper – especially during sale time. Spacious and spread over two floors, there's plenty of room to rifle through the colour-coded racks for items for him, her and the kids, as well as things for the home upstairs.

BOOKS
Agenda Bookshop
Level 0, The Embassy, Santa Lucia Street, Valletta; tel: 2122 7585; June–Sept 9am–midnight, Oct–May Mon–Fri, Sun 9am–10pm, Sat 9am–midnight; map p.132 B2
Literature enthusiasts and bookworms will love it here. The vast selection includes a range of genres,

foreign and local press, top international titles and bestsellers, an expansive travel section, gifts and souvenirs. The Agenda Kids' Club is aimed at 3-to-12-year-olds, and this is the perfect place to bring the children if you're trying to get their head in a book.

Books Plus
Bisazza Street, Sliema; tel: 2133 9400; Mon–Sat 9.30am–7pm; map p.135 E2
Stocks books and magazines, from architecture and art or to building and construction engineering, as well as fiction and just-for-fun titles. Knowledgeable staff will help you find your next favourite read.

Heading to the hills? The **Adventure Camping Shop** (Dun Karm Street Bypass, Birkirkara; tel: 2144 3386; Mon–Fri 9am–7pm, Sat 9am–1pm; map p.135 D1) is the perfect spot to stock up on anything you may need, from sleeping bags to cooking gear, and the friendly and enthusiastic team will teach you everything you need to know.

Left and above left: handmade crafts.

117

Above: searching for lace in Gozo.

HOMEWARES
Cleland & Souchet
Block 14, Level 0, Portomaso, St Julian's; tel: 2138 9898; www.clelandsouchet.com; Mon–Sat 9am–7pm; map p.135 D2

A luxury lifestyle concept born from a wine import company. The collection of brands and services make it a leader in the area, particularly for homeware,

wine, distinctive gifts and fine foods.

Eighteen-Ninety by Camilleri Paris Mode
Annunciation Square, Sliema; tel: 2134 4838; Mon 4.30–7.30pm, Tue–Fri 9.30am–7.30pm, Sat 4.30–6.30pm; map p.135 E2

Get ready to want everything on sale here. Elegant and stylish furnishings for your home, with stocks including decorative ornaments, table linen, fine wines and gourmet food. Renowned for its unusual gifts.

COSMETICS AND PERFUME
Chemimart
20, Republic Street, Valletta; tel: 2124 6063; Mon–Fri 9am–7pm, Sat 9am–8pm; map p.132 B2

A super outlet for prestigious perfumes, cosmetics and toiletries, as well as a

Right: handmade baskets from Gozo.

wide range of health-care products. Stocks well-known brands in a wide range of budgets.

Franks Perfumery
Energy Complex, Republic Street, Valletta; tel: 2124 2579; Mon–Sat 9am–7pm; map.132 B2

The shop for beauty-lovers. Stocks exclusive skincare ranges, up-to-date make-up lines, perfume, cologne and general grooming products. Knowledgeable and helpful staff who are always happy to help.

JEWELLERY
Classic Jewellers
293, Republic Street, Valletta; tel: 2122 0200; Mon–Sat 9am–7pm, Sun 9am–2pm; map p.133 D3

As the name suggests,

expect classic looks including pearl collections, silver, white and yellow gold and intricate filigree. Prices range from affordable to off the radar, but the quality is superbly sleek.

Edwards Lowell Co. Ltd
6–7, Zachary Street, Valletta; tel: 2124 4159; Mon–Fri 9.30am–1pm, 2–7pm, Sat 9.30am–1pm; map p.132 B1 Established in the mid-1920s by an Englishman and offering a selection of watches, jewellery, diamonds and accessories by brands that include Rolex, Podo and Chopard. Book a private appointment and spoil yourself.

Sterling Jewellers
6d Republic Street, Valletta; tel: 2124 4085; Mon–Fri 9am–7pm, Sat 9am–1pm; map p.132 B2 Discover the most beautiful diamonds and luxury

Left: textiles for sale in Gozo.

names in a store that boasts a prestigious portfolio including Gucci, Versace and Dunhill.

Swarovski Premium Store
69, Tower Road, Sliema; tel: 2133 7447; Mon–Sat 10am–7.30pm; map p.135 E2 Step inside this twinkling display of crystal-encrusted items and be dazzled by the sheer shimmer of it all. Choice ranges from classic Swarovski pendants, daring rings, studded wallets and bags to items for the home, as well as more affordable trinkets such as crystal key-rings.

Victor Azzopardi Jewellers
45, Zachary Street, Valletta; tel: 2122 8588; www.victor azzopardi.com; Mon–Fri 9.30am–1pm, 4–7pm, Sat 9.30am–1pm; map p.132 B1 Need something special? Spy the Maltese silver col-

lection and crystal ware or, if you're feeling flash, there's always the diamond collection.

TOYS
Early Learning Centre
193, Merchants Street, Valletta; tel: 2123 6228; Mon–Fri 9am–12.30pm, 4–7pm, Sat 9am–12.30pm; map p.133 C2 Start them young on educational items that promote learning through play. Catering for six years and under, all toys are marked with the trusty 'Early Learning Icon' that details the toy's educational powers.

Pedigree Toyshop
Valletta Waterfront; tel: 2122 6800; daily 9am–9pm; map.133 D1 One of Malta's biggest toy retailers, this chain has been keeping children happy for decades. Items include beach toys, games, dolls and dressing-up gear.

119

Temples

The Maltese Islands' prehistoric temples are easily their most important heritage sites, and tourists flock to them from miles around. Unique throughout the world, this collection of Megalithic structures and underground chambers date from 4000–2500 BC, making them the oldest free-standing formations on the planet. If the distant past fascinates you, there are at least four sites that you'll not want to pass you by – Ggantija, Hagar Qim, Mnajdra and Tarxien – while the underground Ghar Dalam caves also shed light on the fascinating goings-on of prehistory.

Left: Hagar Qim.

PREHISTORIC MALTA AND GOZO

Historic features are dotted all over the Maltese Islands, from the beautiful walled city of Mdina to the numerous towers and buildings constructed by the Knights of St John. But for history and archaeology buffs, none are more important or impressive than the islands' temples – incredible structures that have stood the test of time for millennia. Older than Stonehenge and the Pyramids of Egypt, these temples were built when modern humans (Neolithic farmers) first settled here some 7,000 years ago.

Today, many have argued that these temples should be included as wonders of the world, and many have already been designated as Unesco World Heritage Sites. An ongoing project to protect the two major temples with enormous tents was launched in 2009 and will be extended in 2013.

Ggantija Temples

Temples Street, Xaghra, Gozo; tel: 2155 3194; www.heritage malta.org; daily 9am–5pm with exceptions, last admission 4.30pm; charge; bus: 64, 65; map p.139 C3

One of the most important and mysterious archaeological sites in the world, complete with a stone hearth and altars. Scientific investigation has proved that the Ggantija Temples have stood here for over 6,000 years. The name of the complex is derived from the Maltese word *ggant*, meaning giant.

Ghar Dalam Caves and Museum

Zejtun Road, Birzebbugia; tel: 2165 7419; www.heritage malta.org; daily 9am–5pm with exceptions, last admission 4.30pm; charge; bus: 11, 12, 115; map p.137 D1

An important site that dates settlement in Malta to over 7,400 years ago and which now boasts an underground cave and museum. The number of steps to the location can prove to be an accessibility problem, but otherwise

Left: Ta Hagrat, Mgarr.

malta.org; daily 9am–5pm with exceptions, last admission 4.30pm; charge; bus: 32, 35; map p.136 B1

Probably the most atmospheric of all Malta's temples, the Mnajdra is a complex site consisting of three temples overlooking an oval forecourt. The most impressive includes a largely intact facade and bench constructed in the early Tarxien phase.

Tarxien Temples

Neolithic Temples Street, Tarxien; tel: 2169 5578; www.heritagemalta.org; daily 9am–5pm with exceptions, last admission 4.30pm; charge; bus: 8, 11, 12, 27, 29, 30, 115; map p.137 D3

Dating to between 3600 and 2500 BC, this is the most complex of all temple sites in Malta and consists of four Megalithic structures. A chamber set into the thickness of the wall between the South and Central temples is its most noteworthy feature.

Over the years archaeologists have unearthed fascinating items which helped shed light on the people who built these amazing structures. They have found collections of bones, fragments of pottery and marks of fire that have helped them date settlement in Malta to 5200 BC. Other fantastic finds have included highly decorated stone blocks and screens, reliefs of domestic animals and spirals, a colossal statue and a number of altars, one of which contained a flint knife and animal bones.

3200 BC). Of the elements unearthed at Hagar Qim, notable items include a decorated pillar altar, two table-altars and some 'fat lady' statues now on display in the National Museum of Archaeology, Valletta (see p.85).

Mnajdra Temples

Hagar Qim Road, Qrendi; tel: 2142 4231; www.heritage

this is a fascinating site that all the family will be wowed by.

Hagar Qim

Hagar Qim Road, Qrendi; tel: 2142 4231; www.heritage malta.org; daily 9am–5pm with exceptions, last admission 4.30pm; charge; bus: 32, 35; map p.136 B1

Excavated for the first time in 1839, it dates from the Ggantija phase (c.3600–

Right: Tarxien Temple detail.

Transport

It has to be said that transport on the Maltese Islands still lacks the modernity and reliability of many of its European equivalents, though its vintage yellow buses and classic cars are romantic to look at. Today the small domestic system that is in place consists of public buses and taxis, but plans to revamp it are already under way and will be implemented in the coming few years. While locals are often annoyed by the orange buses and their lack of timekeeping skills, visitors are charmed by these colourful vehicles and the vibrant characters that steer them through Malta's maze of streets.

GETTING TO MALTA

Malta is easily accessible from all over Europe and beyond, with regular flight connections. Airlines flying from the UK to Malta include the national carrier Air Malta, British Airways, Thompson Fly, Thomas Cook, Viking Air and low-cost carriers easyJet and Ryanair. Flights are currently available from most parts of the UK, including London, Birmingham, Manchester, Bristol, Glasgow and Edinburgh.

If you prefer to go overland, you could choose to take a ferry from Italy or Sicily. Ferries currently link Malta to Genoa, Civitavecchia, Catania, Pozzallo and Licata.

GETTING TO GOZO AND COMINO

Malta's sister islands are easily accessible.

The Gozo Ferry, which leaves from Circewwa Har-

bour in Malta and Mgarr Harbour in Gozo, makes the journey every 45 minutes during the day and every one-and-a-half hours or so through the night. It transports cars and passengers, and the crossing takes approximately 25 minutes. For an updated crossing schedule visit: www.gozochannel.com.

Comino is completely car-free, so it's only foot passengers who make the journey across on the little ferry. Ferries are available from Circewwa, Malta, and Mgarr, Gozo.

HIRING A CAR

It's almost impossible to explore the islands to their full potential without a car, and as a result most of the international rental companies have set up shop in Malta too.

Before venturing behind the wheel, it is important to familiarise yourself with driving on the islands. Somewhat surprisingly, Gozo is generally better signposted than the mainland, so map out a journey before you head off. As a country it is one of the few that

Right: Malta's trademark orange bus.

number, while the standard services have two.

Despite their wild service, these buses are generally loved by visitors because of their bright hue and character. Each is usually owned by one driver, who decorates it and makes it his own; in fact it's not unusual to spot a shrine to a religious figure at the front of the bus which is said to help protect it.

For detailed information about the bus timetable and routes visit www.atp.com.mt.

TAXIS AND MINIVANS

Taxis in Malta are split into two categories, black and white: while the black ones have fixed prices for set distances, the white ones don't, and you will need to bargain to get prices down. Hailing a cab isn't the norm in Malta, and it's advised always to carry the number of a reputable firm just in case.

Minibuses are popular locally and ideal if you need to ferry more than five people around at a time. Most local taxi firms also have minivans on offer.

TAXI COMPANIES

It's advisable to book ahead of time if you need a taxi, especially during the summer months.

Freephone Taxis
Tel: 8007 3770 or 2138 9575
Licensed White Taxis
Tel: 2182 3017; email: contact @maltataxi.net
Wembley's
Tel: 2137 4141; email: info@ wembleys.net

The commute into Valletta is often enough to send even the calmest driver over the edge, and traffic can tail back for miles during rush hour. For a more tranquil entrance into the capital, try the ferry from The Strand, Sliema. It leaves regularly and takes about 10 minutes, but do bear the steep climb to the centre of Valletta in mind.

---

follows the British standard of driving on the left, and since their relatively recent introduction, traffic lights have been popping up all over the place trying to slow the feisty Mediterranean driving pace. The same could be said for the increase in speed cameras, so keep your speed down.

CAR HIRE

Car hire can be booked online or at the airport upon arrival. Most hotels also offer special deals on rates, so it's worth checking beforehand.
Drifter
www.driftercarhire.com

Enroute
www.enroutemaltadrive.com
Swansea
www.swanseacarhire.com
Thrifty
www.thrifty.com.mt
Unicar
www.unicarmalta.com

TAKING THE BUS

Admittedly not the most reliable or quick service, Malta's buses are the cheapest and easiest way to navigate round the islands. Except for a few out-of-the-way villages, these bright-orange specimens are well laid out and will get you anywhere and everywhere; most tourist hotspots are particularly well served. Most routes tend to start or end with Valletta, where a massive terminus by City Gate ensures the services tick over. Express options, which bypass the capital and are much quicker, are also available between popular destinations or late at night. As a general rule, the latter routes are marked with a three-digit

Walks and Views

Despite Malta's outwardly built-up appearance, when the heat of the summer stops beating down, ramblers and walkers emerge, keen to make the most of the stunning scenery the islands have to offer. There are numerous spots to explore across the islands, so start by assessing what you'd like to see – dramatic cliffs, lush valleys, scrubland or even the sometimes forgotten backstreets of one of the towns or villages. Views are also abundant. Many of them are breathtaking; you can choose to soak up the Grand Harbour one minute, take in the magnitude of the Mdina Bastions the next, or simply gaze out at the unobstructed Mediterranean.

WALKS

Bahrija Walk
Bus: 65, 80, 81, 86; map p.134 C1
Nigret Roundabout (Rabat) – Bahrija – Mtahleb
The Rabay countryside is beautiful and begs to be explored on foot. It is perfect if you're hoping to happen on views of fertile valleys surrounded by hills and coastal cliffs that even offer a glimpse of the uninhabited island of Filfla.

Highlights of this walk include the site of a Bronze Age village, cliff farmhouses and Roman quarries, as well as Mtahleb's delightful 17th-century chapel. This walk is around 13km (8 miles), and you'll need at least five hours to complete it.

Dwejra Lines Walk
Bus: 43, 44, 45, 50, 65, 86; map p.134 A2–C2
Mgarr – Bingemma – Dwejra – Mosta
A great walk that takes in a mix of rural and urban, culminating in the central

Above: the Red Tower on Marfa Ridge.

town of Mosta. It will take you through arable land to the Speranza Valley, the site of the mysterious Tal-Isperanza Chapel where, legend has it, a girl was saved at the hands of corsairs. Finally, wander through Mosta's busy streets and end up at the world-famous Dome. This walk takes you over 10km (6 miles) and lasts for around four-and-a-half hours.

Girgenti Walk
Bus: 65, 81, 86; map p.136 B2–C1
Buskett (Dingli) – Girgenti – Siggiewi – Qrendi
Enjoy the shade of Malta's only wooden area – Buskett. Wander along by the Roman quarries and, further on, the Inquisitor's 18th-century palace. Siggiewi, which you will reach through the countryside, is also a beautiful village to explore. You'll reach your destination in Il-Maqluba, a large depression in the ground formed by the col-

Right: Gozo's arid landscape.

Left: view of Valetta from Manoel Island.

and crannies that beg to be explored. On the way back to Nadur, you will come across the old watchtower, perched on an elevated part of the village plateau. Allow four hours for this walk.

Marfa Ridge Walk
Bus: 44, 45, 50, 452, 645, 648; map p.134 A4
Ghadira Nature Reserve – Torri L – Ahmar – Immaculate Conception Chapel – Torri L-Abjad – Paradise Bay
Kick off in Mellieha Bay and enjoy the views from the hilltop Red Tower. The solitary Immaculate Conception chapel is one of the highlights, offering stunning views from every angle. Along the route, there are also a number of fortified structures dating back to the days of the Knights of St John, right up to World War II. Bicycle rental is possible from shops in the Mellieha area. Bear in mind that, at certain points, this route may present a physical challenge. In its entirety it will take around five hours and covers 11km (7 miles).

One of the islands' biggest bones of contention is that bird-trapping and hunting are practised in the countryside, and some visitors may find this upsetting. There are, however, strict regulations determining areas where such activities are permitted and times of the year where no such activities are allowed. *See also Environment, p.61.*

lapse of an underground cave. You'll need five hours to complete this walk, especially if you want to fully enjoy the gardens of Buskett, and will cover 12.5km (7½ miles).

Gozo walk
Bus: 42, 43; map p.139 D2
Nadur – Ramla cliffs – Ramla Bay – Nadur
This circular walk starts and ends in the sleepy village of Nadur and takes you through a typical Gozitian valley where traditional agricultural methods can still be observed.
Ramla Bay is a treasure in itself, with stretches of red sand and cave-like nooks

famous because of the breathtaking views visible from it. This tiny cave (which may prove difficult for some to access) overlooks the red sands of Ramla Bay and enjoys unobstructed views of the Gozitan countryside and out to sea.

VIEWS

Azure window, Gozo
Bus: 91; map p.138 A3

An impressive sight and one that has featured in numerous films. This natural arch, formed over thousands of years, is a tranquil spot perfect for a photo opportunity.

Calypso's Cave, Gozo
Bus: 64, 65; map p.139 C3

A popular site made

Dingli Cliffs
Bus: 81, 810; map p.136 A2

A truly impressive sight awaits once you get here: you can look forward to some of the most unbeatable views in the Mediterranean. Dingli Cliffs are Malta's highest point and the island's natural fortress. Take in the striking views and sheerest drops just west of Dingli village, or glance over to the uninhab-

ited island of Filfla. The southwesterly stretch takes in the evocative heights of Buxih, Fawwara, Ghar Lapsi and Munqar, above the sea at Blue Grotto, all of which provide plenty to look at and enjoy.

Mdina Bastions
Bus: 65, 80, 86; map p.134 C1

Having walked through Mdina's alleys, get ready for a spectacular view at the end. The Mdina Bastions offer almost panoramic views of much of the island and are particularly pretty at night. Timed well, it also makes a great spot to watch the *festa* fireworks.

> Always check the weather forecast before heading off, as most routes offer very little protection from the elements. The same goes for protection from the sun – be sure to wear sunglasses, sunscreen and a hat.

St Paul's Island
Bus: 86; map p.134 C3
There's something mysterious and alluring about St Paul's Island. If you don't have time to take a boat over there for a visit, stop to enjoy the view of it instead. The recently completed St Paul's Bay bypass includes a viewing area with benches that makes the ideal resting point.

Upper Barrakka Gardens
All Valletta buses; map p.132 B1

Stick to the designated routes, because a short cut through a privately owned field could be more trouble than it's worth! You'll notice that some rubble walls are marked with blotches of white paint and may also carry the letters RTO. These markings indicate private property.

If you only get to see one stunning view during your time here, make this it. Through this pretty garden you'll find a terrace over-looking the Grand Harbour. It's also a window onto the opposite side where you can see Fort St Angelo and the historic Three Cities.

Valletta from Sliema
Bus: 61, 63, 65, 70, 627, 645, 652; map p.135 E2
Standing at the Sliema Ferries, you are privy to the spectacular view of the Valletta Bastions, built by the Knights of St John. Take a boat out through the harbour to get a closer look.

Wine

Like most things here, local wine is all about passion and history. In fact, the local viticulture industry can be traced back to Phoenician times. Back then, the Mediterranean offered perfect grape-growing conditions, and as a result the Maltese people continued to grow grapes for the Romans and later for the Knights of St John who revived the industry. To this day, production is still going strong, with wines of unique Maltese character taking hold and red, white and rose varieties produced. Many winemaking companies offer tours of their cellars and production houses, with wine-tasting events held afterwards.

WINEMAKING

With a history dating back thousands of years, winemaking in Malta has plenty to live up to. The modern industry started around 1920, but it wasn't until the early 1970s that an local wine industry began in earnest. Until then, most grapes grown locally were indigenous table varieties; however, recent initiatives including the 'Vines for Wine' campaign launched by the government, have encouraged farmers to take up viticulture by offering them training and financial support. This has sparked interest, and as a result small fields have been transformed into vineyards. But although the demand for local vineyard production outstrips supply, it won't be too long before more of the Maltese countryside is covered with vineyards. Currently, any shortfall in grapes is made up by imported quality grapes from northern Italy and France.

Above: Gozo wines.

Malta may not be as renowned for wine production as its larger Mediterranean neighbours, but Maltese vintages are now happily holding their own at international competitions and have recently won several accolades in France, Italy and further afield. Today, the major wineries have invested heavily in the latest technology and training to better their product.

International grape varieties grown here include Cabernet Sauvignon, Merlot, Syrah, Grenache, Sauvignon Blanc, Chardonnay, Carignan, Chenin Blanc and Moscato. The most common grape varieties are local specialities: Gellewza, Gennarua and Ghirghentina. The biggest boost for the local industry to date was the introduction of the quality wine system DOK (Denominazzjoni ta' Origini Kontrollata) in 2007. Look out for the DOK label when purchasing wine so as to be sure that you are buying a 100 percent local product.

VINEYARDS AND WINEMAKERS

Malta has a number of local winemakers who are proud of their produce. Whether you're a wine connoisseur or simply interested in sampling some local varieties, then why not arrange a visit to one of the vineyards in Malta, where you can experience how wine is made and even get to taste the various flavours?

Emmanuel Delicata Winemaker
The Winery, Ix-Xatt, Paola; tel: 2182 5199; www.delicata.com;

days and Thursdays, but booking is essential.

Meridiana Wine Estate

National Park, Ta' Qali; tel: 2141 5301; www.meridiana.com.mt; map p.135 C1

In the heart of a beautiful wine estate, you'll be taken on a tour and given plenty of tasty varieties to try. By appointment only.

Montekristo Vineyards

The Winery, Hal Farrug, l/o Siggiewi; tel: 2123 1448; www.montekristo.com; map p.136 B2

A typical visit includes an introductory film, guided tour of the winery and vaults, and an opportunity to taste and purchase Montekristo wines at the on-site wine shop.

If you don't consider yourself much of a wine connoisseur, why not try **local beer**? Farsons is famous for Cisk lager and you can enjoy a two-hour brewery tour that really puts you in the picture of how it goes from hops to bottled at this central brewing house and the bottling hall. Tours cost €4.66 per person. To book call 2381 4114.

are pressed, fermented and eventually transformed into wine, and finally a selection of wines to taste accompanied by local savoury snacks. Tours are held on Tues-

by appointment only; map p.135 E1

Enjoy a tutored wine-tasting or educational training session in the 17th-century cellar, where oak fermentation and maturation takes place in 225-litre French and American barrels.

Marsovin

The Winery, Wills Street, Marsa; tel: 2182 4918; www.marsovin winery.com; map p.135 E1

The tour commences with a historical introduction, followed by an explanation about the process of how the locally grown grapes

Right: Marsovin vineyards.

Atlas

The following maps of
Malta, Gozo and Comino make it
easy to find the attractions listed in
our A–Z section. A selective index to
streets and sights will help you find
other locations throughout the city.

Map Legend

Pedestrian area		★	Sight of interest
Notable building		ℹ	Tourist information
Park		🏰	Castle / fort
Hotel		⁂	Ancient site
Urban area		✉	Post office
Non urban area		⛪	Cathedral / church
Transport Hub		☾	Mosque
Ferry route		†	Monastery
✈ Airport		🕳	Cave
🚌 Bus station		ᴍ̂	Museum/gallery
🗼 Lighthouse		🎭	Theatre/concert hall
⚲ Beach		📖	Library
☀ View point		🗽	Statue / monument
▲ Peak		✚	Hospital

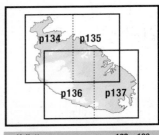

p134	p135
p136	p137

Valletta	p132 – 133
Gozo	p138 – 139

Valletta

Manoel
Island

↑ Sliema

4

Il-Port Ta' Marsamxett
(Marsamxett Harbour)

St Sebastian
Bastion

Au
de Ba

German
Curtain

*Water Polo
Pitch*

Auberge
d'Aragon

Archbishop's
Palace

3

St Salvatore
Bastion

Siege Road

St Andrew's
Bastion

Triq L-Assedju L-Kbir (Great

St Paul's
Cathedral

Our Lady
of Carmel

Manoel
Theatre

Pjazza
Mattia Preti

Misrah
San Gorg

St Michael's
Bastion

Gran
Master
Palac

Misrah
Ir-Repubblika

National Museum
of Fine Arts

St Augustine

Law Courts

Misrah Ir-
Assedju L-Kbir
(Great Siege Square)

Mal
Libra

2

Osborne
Hotel

Auberge de Provence
Museum of Archaeology

St John's
Co-Cathedral

Palazzo
di Città

St P
Shipy

St Andrew

Toy
Museum

Pjazza San Gwann
(St John's Square)

Embassy of the
Order of St John

St Francis

St John's
Cavalier

HASTING'S
GARDEN

St Barbara

St James

Palazzo
Ferreria

Hotel
Castille

Royal Opera
House
(site of)

St Catherine

Auberge
d'Italie

Grand
Harbour
Hotel

Vi
Ga

1

City Gate

Triq Ir-Repubblika

Our Lady
of Victories

N

St James
Cavalier Centre
for Creativity

Auberge de
Castille et Leon

Triton
Fountain

UPPER
BARRAKKA
GARDENS

Our Lady
of Liesse

Central
Bank

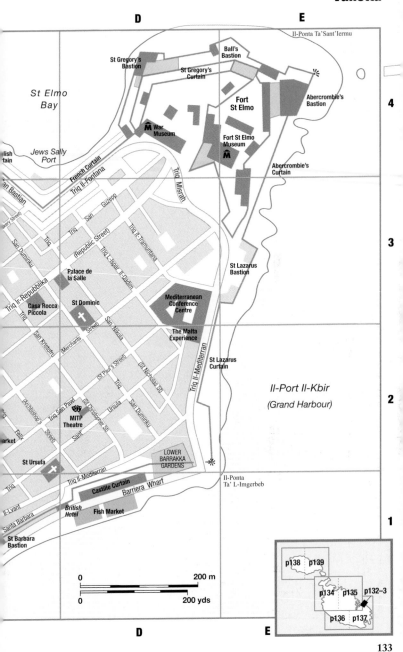

D   **E**

Il-Ponta Ta'Sant'Iermu

St Gregory's
Bastion

Ball's
Bastion

St Gregory's
Curtain

*St Elmo
Bay*

Fort
St Elmo

Abercrombie's
Bastion

4

War
Museum

Fort St Elmo
Museum

*Jews Sally
Port*

Abercrombie's
Curtain

lish
tain

French Curtain

an Bastian

Triq Il-Fontana

Triq Misraħ

kery Street)

Triq

Triq San Ġużepp

St Lazarus
Bastion

3

San Duminku

Triq

(Republic Street)

Triq L-Isqof Tt Qadim

Triq L-Isqof Tt Qadim

Triq Ir-Repubblika

Triq

Palace de
la Salle

St Dominic

Mediterranean
Conference
Centre

Casa Rocca
Piccola

St Nikola

Triq

The Malta
Experience

San Kristofru

(Merchants)   Street)

(St Paul's Street)

(St Nicholas St)

St Lazarus
Curtain

Triq Il-Mediterran

Il-Port Il-Kbir

(Grand Harbour)

2

(Archbishop's)

Triq San Pawl

MITP
Theatre

St Christopher St)

San Duminku

Felix
Street

St Ursula

LOWER
BARRAKKA
GARDENS

Il-Ponta
Ta' L-Imgerbeb

Castile Curtain

Triq Il-Mediterran

Barriera Wharf

1

Il-Lvant

British
Hotel

Fish Market

Santa Barbara

St Barbara
Bastion

0   200 m

0   200 yds

D   **E**

A   **B**

4

Il-Fliegu ta' Malta (South Comino Channel)

White Tower
Ponta ta'l-Ahrax (Ahrax Point)

Armier Bay

Vendôme Battery

Madonna 44
Madonna Statue

Ponta tal-Marfa (Marfa Point)

Cirkewwa
Ramla Bay
Kortin it-Twil

Dahlet ix-Xilep

Paradise Bay

Marfa

Eskalar Redoubt

Il-Parsott

L-Ahrax tal Ghajn

Rdum il-Qawwi

Ta'Imgharrqa

Ras il-Qammieh

Red Tower

Mellieha Bay

Ras-il-Griebeg

Selmun Bay

St Paul's Statue

Ras il-Quammieh (Qammieh Point)

Ghadira Beach

Marfa Ridge

3

Ic-Cumnija   Biskra

Il-Qortin ta' Ghajn Zeftuna

Qawra Tower

Fort Campbell

St Paul's Statue

Ras in-Niexfa

Il-Hofra

Statue of St Paul

Tal-Blata

St Paul's Islands

Redoubt
Ras il-Mignuna

Il-Prajjet (Anchor Bay)

Popeye Village

Mellieha

Selmun Palace

Mellieha Fort

Mistra Bay

Bugi

Ghadira Bay

Rdum id-Delli

Xemxija

Ghajn Znuber Tower

Mellieha Ridge

St Paul's Bay

Neolithic Tombs

Mizieb

Is-Simar

St Paul's Bay

Victory

Pwales

Ta' Rkuplu

Tal-Qadi Temple

Ras il-Wahx

Manikata

Ta'l Argentier

Pwales Valley

Ghajn Astas

In-Nahhalija

St George

San Martin

Wardija   Bur

2

Ramla tal-Mixquqa (Golden Bay)

Ghajn Tuffieha

Il-Palma

St Martin

Gebel Ghawzara 116

Ghajn Tuffieha Bay

Il-Fawwara

Wardija Ridge

Il-Qoll

Ta' Brare

Ta' Ghajn Tuffieha Tower

Il-Karraba

Roman Baths

Ta' Zerb

St Margar

Gnejna Bay

Ghajn Tuffieha

Hal Dragu

Ras il-Pellegrin

Lippia Tower

Zammitello Palace

Skorba Temples

Bidnija Hill

Ta' Zammitello

Mgarr

Zebbieh

Il-Pellegrin 127

Ta Hagrat Temples

Gnejna

L-Iskorvit

Bingemma

Bezbezija

Fommir-Rih Bay

Ta'l-Abatija

Tas-Santi

Victoria Lines

Ras ir-Raheb

Mgarr

Bingemma Fort

Dwejra Lines

Tal-Oleigha

Dwejra

Kuncizz

1

Bronze Age Village

St Martin

Hotba ta' San Martin 214

Nadur Tower

Roman Catacombs & Prehistoric Tombs

Il-Gattara

Buqana

Nat Sta

Wied tal-Bahrija

Ghemieri Palace

Tas-Salib

Chadwick Lakes

Mtarla Clock Tower

Mtarfa

Malta Avia Mus

Rdum tal-Vigarju

Bahrija

Ghemieri

Fiddien Reservoir

Gnien is-Sultan

Roman Villa

Mdina   Ma

Tal Merhla 212

Is-Sentini

Ghajn Klieb

Cathedral

St Augustine

Rdum tas-Sarg

L-Andrijet

Nigred

St Paul

Rabat

St Agatha's Church

St Paul's Catacombs

Migra Ferha

Ta' Laknija

Underground Chapel

Dominican Monastery

Ta'-V

Ta' Baldu 189

Mtahleb

Hotret ir-Rizz

Ta' Dekozzu

Gnien il-Kbir

Ta' Baldu

A   **B**

136

p138 p139

p134 p135

p136 p137

N

0   2 km

0   1 mile

4

M E D I T E R R A N E A N

S E A

3

wra
wer

Ras il-Qawra
(Qawra Point)

Ras il-Ghallis
(Ghallis Point)

wra

Ghallis Rocks

Salina
Bay

il-Hotba
ns

**Ghallis
Tower**

*Qalet
Marku*

Ras il-Qrejten
(Qrejten Point)

**Annuncia
ichael**

Ta' Hammud

St Mark's Tower

**Qadi
ple**

Bahar
ic-Caghaq

Il Blata l-Bajda

Splash and Fun Water Park

Madliena
Tower

Maghtab

Ras l-Irqieqa

St John

Ta' San Pietru

**Madliena
Fort**

**Pembroke
Fort**

St George's
Tower

chael

St Catherine

Madliena

Il Ponta tad-Dragunara
(Dragonara Point)

2

Mosta Fort

San Pawl
tat-Targa

Gharghur

Il-Mielah

Paceville

St Julian's

Casino

rah
mob

St Margaret

**Church of the
Assumption
(Mosta Dome)**

Nexxar

Tal-Mejda

Il-Qaliet

Spinola Palace

St Julian's Point

*Balluta
Bay*

St Julian's Tower

Sliema Point
Tower

St Anton

Ta' Giorni

Msierah

Ta' Raddiena

Ta' Gwann
tal-Gharghar

Mosta

Dia

L-Iklin

Sacred Heart

Gzira

Stella Maris

Sliema

Siracusa, Napoli

umbo
ower

Balzan

St Helen

University

Sliema Creek

Tigne Fort

Dragut Point

Manoel Island Harbour

**Fort
Manoel**

**St Elmo
Lighthouse**

Ta' Qali

Tal-Mirakli

Birkirkara

Is-Swatar

Ta' Xbiex

Marsamxett

Valletta

Ricasoli Point

Pumping
Station

**San Anton Palace
and Gardens**

Msida

**Argotti Botanical
Gardens**

**Ricasoli
Fort**

p132-3

Qali
fts Village

Attard

Santa
Venera

Grand Harbour

**Fort
St Angelo**

Pinella

toria

Ta' Qassati

Gwardamanga

Vittoriosa

Kalkara

Ta' Sari Gwakkin

Il-Kortin

**Inquisitor's
Palace**

**Mt. Carmel
Hospital**

Wied is Sewda

Il-Hofor

Hamrun

St Lawrence

**Our Lady
of Victories**

Cospicua

**Ta' Srina
James**

Il-Hammieri

Marsa

Senglea

Kordin

Cottonera Lines

Zebbug

Tal-Hlas

Qorm

**Our Lady of
All Graces**

**De Rohan
Arch**

Hal Muxi

Tal-Hlas

Ghar Ram

Ghammieri

St Vincent de
Paule Hospital

Paola

**Christ
the King**

**Homepesch
Arch**

1

St Philip

Hal Mola

Tal-Handaq

Hypogeum

Fgura

Tarxien Temples

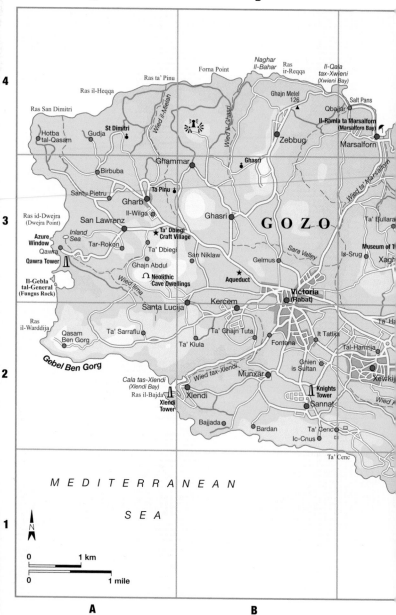

A

4

Ras il-Heqqa

Ras San Dimitri

Hotba
tal-Qasam

Gudja

St Dimitri

Ras ta' Pinu

Forna Point

*Naghar
Il-Bahar*

Ras
ir-Reqqa

*Il-Qala
tax-Xwieni
(Xwieni Bay)*

Ghajn Melel
126

Qbajjar

Salt Pans

**Il-Ramla ta Marsalforn
(Marsalforn Bay)**

Zebbug

Marsalforn

Birbuba

Ghammar

Ghasri

Santu Pietru

Gharb

Ta Pinu

Il-Wilga

Ghasri

3

Ras id-Dwejra
(Dwejra Point)

San Lawrenz

*Inland
Sea*

**Azure
Window**

Tar-Rokan

★ **Ta' Dbiegi
Craft Village**

Ta' Dbiegi

San Niklaw

G O Z O

Ta' Bullara

Museum of T

Is-Srug

Xagh

**Qawra
Qawra Tower**

Sara Valley

Gelmus

**Il-Gebla
tal-General
(Fungus Rock)**

Ghajn Abdul

Ω **Neolithic
Cave Dwellings**

★ **Aqueduct**

**Victoria
(Rabat)**

Wied Ilma

Santa Lucija

Kercem

Ras
il-Warddija

Qasam
Ben Gorg

Ta' Sarraflu

Ta' Ghajn Tuta

Fontana

It Tatlija

Ta' Ha

Tal-Hannija

Gebel Ben Gorg

Ta' Klula

Gnien
is Sultan

Xewki

2

*Cala tas-Xlendi
(Xlendi Bay)*

Ras il-Bajda

Wied tax-Xlendi

Munxar

**Xlendi
Tower**

Xlendi

**Knights
Tower**

Sannat

Wied

Bajjada

Bardan

Ta' Cenc

Ic-Cnus

1

M E D I T E R R A N E A N

S E A

N

Ta' Cenc

0   1 km

0   1 mile

A   B

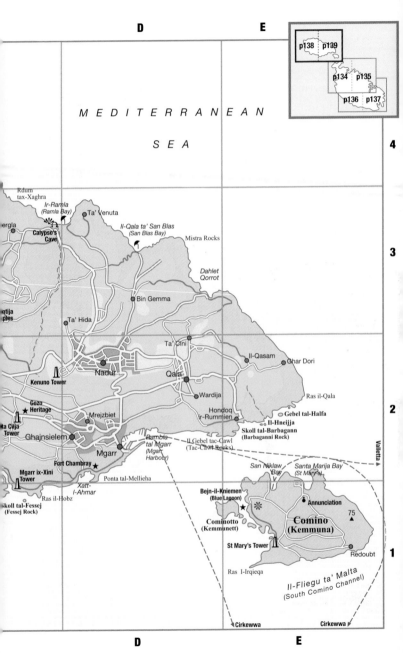

MEDITERRANEAN

SEA

4

Rdum tax-Xaghra

Ir-Ramla
(Ramla Bay)

Ta' Venuta

Il-Qala ta' San Blas
(San Blas Bay)

Mistra Rocks

ergla

Calypso's
Cave

3

Dahlet
Qorrot

ntija
ples

Bin Gemma

Ta' Hida

Ta' Cini

Il-Qasam

Ghar Dori

Nadur

Qala

Kenuno Tower

Wardija

Ras il-Qala

Goza
Heritage

Mrejzbiet

Hondoq
ir-Rummien

Gebel tal-Halfa

2

ta Cilja
Tower

Il-Hneijja

Skoll tal-Barbagann
(Barbaganni Rock)

Ghajnsielem

Mgarr

Rambla
tal Mgarr
(Mgarr
Harbour)

Il Gebel tac-Cawl
(Tac-Cawl Rocks)

Fort Chambray

Valletta

Mgarr ix-Xini
Tower

Ponta tal-Mellieha

Xatt-
l-Ahmar

San Niklaw
Bay

Santa Marija Bay
(St Mary's)

koll tal-Fessej
(Fessej Rock)

Ras il-Hobz

Bejn-il-Kniemen
(Blue Lagoon)

Annunciation

Cominotto
(Kemmunett)

Comino
(Kemmuna)

75

St Mary's Tower

Redoubt

1

Ras I-Irqieqa

Il-Fliegu ta' Malta
(South Comino Channel)

Cirkewwa

Cirkewwa

Index

143

Insight Smart Guide: Malta
Written by: **Jo Caruana**
Proofread and indexed by: **Neil Titman**
Photography by: **Sylvaine Poitau/APA** except: Alamy 61B; Aurora Opera House 51B; Ian Bellinger/fotoLibra 86/87B; Fortina Spa Resort 99B; Fotolia 3T; Fuego 96B; Mario Galea & MTV Networks International 95T; Glyn Genin/APA 91B; The Grand Hotel Excelsior 98C; iStockphoto.com 36C, 36/37, 55T, 58B, 59B, 60B, 63B; Leonardo 41B, 100B; Maltaqua 56/57; Jeremy de Maria 55L; melmif photography 3CR, 97; Mario Micallef/ Maltaqua 57B; Nove 94B; Radisson Hotels & Resorts 80T, 100T; RIU Hotels & Resorts 80B, 98/99T; Joe Smith 55T; Tony Spiteri 91T; Magda Spiteri/fotoLibra 54B; The Victoria Hotel 4B, 78T; Darin Zammit Lupi 50/51
Picture Manager: **Steven Lawrence**
Maps: **James Macdonald, Phoenix**

Mapping
Series Editor: **Jason Mitchell**

First Edition 2010
© 2010 Apa Publications GmbH & Co. Verlag KG Singapore Branch, Singapore.
Printed in Singapore by Insight Print Services (Pte) Ltd

Worldwide distribution enquiries:
Apa Publications GmbH & Co. Verlag KG (Singapore Branch) 38 Joo Koon Road, Singapore 628990; tel: (65) 6865 1600; fax: (65) 6861 6438

Distributed in the UK and Ireland by:
GeoCenter International Ltd
Meridian House, Churchill Way West, Basingstoke, Hampshire RG21 6YR;
tel: (44 1256) 817 987; fax: (44 1256) 817 988

Distributed in the United States by:
Langenscheidt Publishers, Inc.
36–36 33rd Street 4th Floor, Long Island City, New York 11106; tel: (1 718) 784 0055; fax: (1 718) 784 0640l

Contacting the Editors
We would appreciate it if readers would alert us to errors or outdated information by writing to:
Apa Publications, PO Box 7910, London SE1 1WE, UK; fax: (44 20) 7403 0290;
e-mail: insight@apaguide.co.uk

Malta Bus Routes

Direct Services
Route Number

22	Cospicua to Marsascala and vice versa
23	Cospicua to Xghajra and vice versa
48	Bugibba/Qawra to Cirkewwa via Ghadira and vice versa
51	Bugibba/Qawra to Ghajn Tuffieha and vice versa
65	Sliema Ferry to Rabat via St. Julian's, Taz-Zwejt, Mosta and Ta' Qali
70	Sliema Ferry to Bugibba/Qawra via Coast road and vice versa
86	Bugibba to Rabat via Mosta and Ta' Qali and vice versa
94	Siggiewi to Ghar Lapsi and vice versa (Sun. and Thurs.- summer only)
98	Valletta "Circular"
427	Bugibba/Qawra to Marsaxlokk via 3 cities and vice versa
627	Bugibba/Qawra to Marsaxlokk via Sliema and 3 cities, and vice versa
645	Sliema Ferry to Cirkewwa and vice versa
652	Sliema Ferry to Golden Bay via Bugibba/Qawra and Ghajn Tuffieha Bay, and vice versa